People Skills for Christians

How to Change Behaviors
That Sabotage Believers' Lives

Tony Munson

Copyright © 2017 by Tony Munson

All rights reserved. Written permission must be secured from the author to use or reproduce any part of this book, except for brief quotations in critical reviews or articles.

The author may be contacted through his website at www.effectivelivingllc.com.

Scripture quotations taken from the Amplified® Bible (AMP). Copyright © 2015 by The Lockman Foundation. Used by permission. www.Lockman.org.

Scripture quotations taken from the Amplified® Bible (AMPC). Copyright © 1954, 1958, 1962, 1964, 1965, 1987 by The Lockman Foundation. Used by permission. www.Lockman.org.

Scripture taken from *The Message*. Copyright © 1993, 1994, 1995, 1996, 2000, 2001, 2002. Used by permission of NavPress Publishing Group.

Scripture taken from the New King James Version®. Copyright © 1982 by Thomas Nelson. Used by permission. All rights reserved.

THE HOLY BIBLE, NEW INTERNATIONAL VERSION®, NIV®. Copyright © 1973, 1978, 1984, 2011 by Biblica, Inc®. Used by permission. All rights reserved worldwide.

Scripture quotations marked (NLT) are taken from the Holy Bible, New Living Translation. Copyright © 1996, 2004, 2007 by Tyndale House Foundation. Used by permission of Tyndale House Publishers, Inc., Carol Stream, Illinois 60188. All rights reserved.

The Living Bible. Copyright © 1971 by Tyndale House Foundation. Used by permission of Tyndale House Publishers, Inc., Carol Stream, Illinois 60188. All rights reserved.

ISBN-13: 978-1540859174
ISBN-10: 1540859177

To the millions of Christians out there who have *huge* hearts
but lack the necessary skills to overcome the people problems
they face in their daily lives and ministries

and

To you—
the person who's about ready to unlock
an untapped reservoir of potential for your life

Contents

Foreword .... *ix*
Acknowledgments .... *xiii*
Introduction .... *xv*

Part 1: Laying the Foundation

Chapter 1: The HUGE Opportunity Available to Us 3
   The Opportunity Tree 5
   Our Potential Pie 7
   People Are the Gatekeepers of Our Opportunities 13

Chapter 2: You and God Are a Team 15

Chapter 3: How We Get Results 21
   What We See, Read, and Hear 22
   What We Think about and Believe 26
   What We Say and Do 27
   Our Results 29

Chapter 4: Your Thought Life Determines Your Reality 31
   Reprogram Your Thought Life 31
   Our Thoughts Produce Actions 34

Chapter 5: The Power of "Do" 37
   Knowledge Is Only Potential Power 37
   All of the Power Is in the "Do" 39

Chapter 6: People Are Predictable 43
   People Like to Be "Operated" a Specific Way 44
   Most People Are Only Concerned with Themselves 45

Chapter 7: The Law of Sowing and Reaping 49

If You Don't Want Corn, Don't Plant Corn Seeds 50
What's in Your Garden? 51
Get Some Good Seeds in the Ground 52
Be Patient 53
Chapter 8: Selfishness Is at the Root of Most Problems 55
Chapter 9: Learn to Love People 61
The New Commandment 63
God's Definition of Love 64
Love Is a Choice 65
Let God Change You from the Inside 66
Chapter 10: The Golden Rule 69
Chapter 11: The Power of Words 71
Death and Life 72
Our Mouths Are Weapons 75
Words Are Seeds 75
Our Mouths Are the Steering Wheels of Our Lives 76
Our Faith Comes by Words We Hear 77
Chapter 12: We Have a "Bank Account" with Every Person We Meet 79

Part 2: Concrete Application

Chapter 13: The Three "Do Nots" 87
Do Not Criticize People 87
Do Not Gossip 91
Do Not Complain 95
Chapter 14: How to Correct People 99
Does It Matter If They Are Wrong? 100
Correct People in Private, If Possible 101
Focus on the Behavior, Not the Person 103
Cushion the Blow 104

Chapter 15: The Power of a Question.................................. 107
   Include People in the Solution 108
Chapter 16: Appreciate People and Make Them Feel Important . 111
   Appreciation Motivates People... 112
   Appreciation Should Be a Lifestyle 113
   Tangible Gifts 115
   Initiate Interactions with People 117
Chapter 17: Get to Know Others... 119
   What's Important to Them?.. 120
   Make Yourself Available 121
   The Power of Lunch 122
Chapter 18: Handling Conversation 125
   Set the Tone of Your Conversation 125
   Get the Focus off of You.. 126
   Ask Questions 128
Chapter 19: How to Be a Better Listener 131
   Are You Really Listening?... 132
   Listen with Your Body... 133
   Don't Interrupt... 136
   Give Vocal Queues 138
   Demonstrate You Understand 138
   Don't Hijack the Conversation... 139
Chapter 20: A Happy Countenance.. 141
   Smile... 142
   What Do You Think about All Day? 143
Chapter 21: The Power of Names 149
   Just Ask 150
   Demonstrate People Are Important to You 150
   Names Personalize Interactions... 151

    The "Million-Dollar Test"... *152*
    Tips for Remembering More Names...................................... *153*
Chapter 22: Motivating People... 155
    Find Out What's Important to a Person *158*
    Talk about Why It's Beneficial to the Other Person *160*
Chapter 23: Dealing with Conflict... 163
    Never Argue *165*
    Admit Your Mistakes and Apologize, If Necessary *167*
    Ask Questions *169*
    If You Have a Problem with Someone, Go Talk to That Person ... *170*
    Choose Not to Be Offended *173*
    Forgive... *179*
Chapter 24: Communication and Technology 185
    Effective Communication Results from Human Contact............ *185*
    Technology Makes Us Feel Anonymous *187*
    The Internet Never Forgets *188*
Chapter 25: How Do We Get Better?... 191
    Look for Opportunities... *191*
    Continue Learning *193*
    Set Up Systems to Enforce Good Behavior............................. *195*
Conclusion *197*
Afterword.. *198*
How to Be Born Again *199*
Bibliography... *202*

Foreword

"**W**hy are you writing this book?" you ask. Well, as I started digging into material related to people skills (soft skills or interpersonal skills), I immediately noticed a huge missing skill set in the Christian church as a whole. To put it bluntly, many Christians lack the necessary skill set required to reach the lost (non-Christians) and maintain a healthy church body. The more I learned, the more I became convinced that Christians and Christian churches could be better positioned for success if they knew what I had learned—how to get along with people more effectively (more specifically, how to avoid and resolve conflict, deal with offense, build stronger relationships to increase opportunities, and have a more healthy influence over others—just to name a few). Coupled with my Christian background, I realized I could be just the person to help educate my fellow believers in this underdeveloped area.

What you are holding in your hands is the result of literally hundreds and hundreds of hours of reading, praying, teaching and mentoring people, listening to teachings, and hands-on application. Each chapter and section has been specifically selected because of the usefulness of the principles it contains. Every attempt has been made to remove filler, too. I'm a results kind of guy. If something isn't helping me, at best it's doing nothing for me, which means it needs to be evaluated. At worst, it's hurting me; and in that case, it needs to go. I have not only found all of the concepts in this book to be helpful from a personal standpoint but also from a mentoring perspective—they are changing people's lives. To the best of my ability, I have trimmed out the "fluff" and only included concepts that have some "meat" to them.

How is this book different from all of the other people skills books available? Well, for starters, this is a book written by a Christian, for Christians. I don't dance around the Bible or the fact that there is a God and that He does love you. I'm not out to try to appeal to the largest audience possible, so I don't feel like I need to hide God from the reader. This is family business here. I use relevant secular (not religious) material and Scripture together to give you the best picture of how you can be more skillful with those around you.

My intent is to make this book *the* definitive resource for how Christians should relate to each other (and to the rest of the world, as a matter of fact)—a guide to becoming a "civilized" believer. As Christians, we are supposed to set an example for the rest of the world to follow. Sadly, many Christians and Christian churches fail in this regard because they don't understand some of the most fundamental spiritual and interpersonal laws necessary to succeed. In the pages of this book are concrete principles you can build your life on. They work for me. They work for the people I teach. They absolutely will work for you—if you do them.

This book is designed to bridge the gap between the teachings you're receiving at church (and reading in the Bible) and the people you interact with every single day. If you're like me, sometimes I walk away from a great church service wondering to myself, "How exactly can I apply that to my life?" Jesus told us (in John 13:34) that we are to love each other. What does that look like in real life, where the rubber meets the road? This book is designed to answer that question by giving you concrete skills to use when loving people in your life. It's meant to be a book of practical application—a supplement to the spiritual teaching you're hopefully already receiving.

God is in the "people business"; and if you're a Christian, so are you. As a Christian, your new, full-time job is to have a closer relationship with God and to help Him accomplish His will in the world. The ultimate purpose of every single thing God is doing in the earth today is to help people—help bring them into the kingdom, help them live better lives, help give them a safe church environment in which to grow—and that's nowhere near an exhaustive list of the help people need! If you want to be better at your true career, you need training. To be the most effective in every area of our lives, we must have the necessary skills to properly lead and influence others. No amount of prayer will make up for continually violating the laws of interpersonal communication.

I believe trying to change any Christian without using God's Word and leading as the primary instruments is like trying to mow your grass with a pair of scissors—it can be done, but it's a lot harder than if you just used the mower sitting in your garage. As Christians, we need to use *all* of the tools at our disposal. God's Word has the power to permanently change our hearts, and that's exactly what many of us need when it comes to being better with people—a heart transplant. This book, combined with the Word of God, will help give you the foundational skills you need to properly walk out God's kind of love each and every day.

Some people are going to be challenged by the things I've written, and that is a good thing! Many Christians are living far below their potential because of their own self-destructive behaviors. I can't address every behavior, but I can address our people skills—which, based on my experience, are literally (and figuratively) *killing* Christians and Christian churches all over the country. Enough is enough! It's time for us to get good at the fundamentals, so we can move on to the bigger and better things God has for our lives.

Acknowledgments

I would like to thank the following people for their help and guidance. Without them, this book wouldn't even be a thought in the most distant recesses of my brain.

God—*Whose written Word has transformed me from the inside out.*

Stephanie, my wife—*For keeping me grounded and volunteering to take this wild ride through life with me. If this book makes any sense whatsoever, thank her—she edited it!*

Pastor Mark Boer—*Without his spiritual leadership, my life wouldn't look anything like it does today—and I like my life!*

Joe Argon—*We started on the personal-growth journey together and have been sharpening each other ever since.*

My mom—*Who introduced me to God at a young age and forever changed the course of my life. She taught me the way I should go, and I did later return.*

Introduction

Congratulations! If you're reading this book, I assume you are a born-again Christian, and your eternity is no longer in question. You have experienced one of the greatest miracles ever performed—moving from spiritual death to spiritual life. You are right with God, and no other human accomplishment on this planet can even come close to what has taken place. You are accepted by God, have all of His promises available to you, and even have access to the refrigerator!

If you haven't been born again or are not sure if you have (or what that even means), what's the holdup? When you die (and you will) and leave your body (and you will), will you really be surprised to find out that God actually does exist? Think about that for a moment. I don't think you'll be surprised. I suspect you will have an uh-oh, they-were-right moment; but by then, it'll be too late. If you already believe in God to some degree, why not make sure your eternity is secure by following the instructions God gave concerning *how* to be saved? Believing God exists is a great start, but it doesn't get you there. You can have an I-know-for-sure experience right here, right now, wherever you are reading this book. If I'm describing you, please turn to the back of this book to take care of business and then come right back. It won't take long. You have everything to gain.

OK, good, we are all on the same team now. From here on out, I'll be talking to you like we are family—because we are now!

YOUR LACK OF SKILL WITH PEOPLE IS ROBBING YOU OF HAPPINESS, HEALTH, AND FINANCIAL PROSPERITY

The better your relationships are, the happier you are. Better relationships means less stress and the laundry list of physical problems associated with it. Better relationships means more opportunities—both financial and relational. A church full of individuals who are good with

~~people is more effective at reaching and~~ training others, and ~~keeping the local church healthy. Christians with strong people skills also are more effective at preaching the gospel (sharing the good news about Jesus), because they avoid many of the common communication pitfalls that create barriers between them and their listeners.~~

~~Just like there are physical laws that govern the universe, there are laws of communication that govern our interactions with each other: Violate them, and you won't get the desired result. Many of us have poor communication skills and don't even realize it—we were never taught.~~ The good news is there are best practices for dealing with people, so we don't have to start from scratch. Sometimes, we just need to be reminded of the basics. Remember, just because you've heard something before doesn't mean you know it. Our goal is to take the material we're going to talk about and move it from our heads to our hearts. Some of the principles in this book will immediately start affecting your relationships in a positive way.

I want to put more tools in your tool belt that you can use to yield positive results when interacting with your friends, family, and fellow Christians. This book is about using tried and true fundamentals to communicate with and motivate the people around you. When strained relationships are present, we are not getting the best out of each other—how can we or our organizations reach our potential under such circumstances?

This book will give you options to grow, maintain, and fix the relationships in your life. If people lack options, they will default to the tools they have—which, for many people, aren't working that great for them right now. After reading this book, you'll be able to recognize a particular situation and know immediately how to respond without having to fly by the seat of your pants. There is a better way! You can intelligently manage the interactions in your life, instead of constantly feeling like you are at the mercy of circumstances that are out of your control.

We were not born with great people skills, unfortunately. While it's true that some people seem to have more of a natural knack with people, the only real difference between them and others is they have naturally identified some of the rules we are going to talk about in this book, and they follow them to their own benefit. You can and will be a great people person if you apply what we'll talk about. The potential is there; with a little training, we can bring it out.

Like anything else in life, the results you get will be proportionate to the amount of effort you put in. If you read this book, pat yourself on the back, and say, "Wow, sure was a nice read" and then go right back to the way you've currently been interacting with people, you will see very little benefit. If you decide to change, and I'll do my best to convince you that you should, you *will* see the fruit of your labor. You're going to be *somewhere* five years from now—why not increase the quality of your life instead of running on the hamster wheel some more?

If people problems follow you around wherever you go, *you* might be the problem. I know this is difficult for some people to hear, but the reason you are not satisfied with the relationships in your life might be because *you* are the source of the dissatisfaction. If you're tired of friction, feeling alienated, and dealing with the same reoccurring problems, it might not be because everyone else needs to change. It might be because you need to change. Be mature enough to consider that you might be doing something that's contributing to the problem.

As a fellow Christian, I have a vested interest in you becoming an amazing people person. People don't leave a church because of problems with God; they leave a church because of problems with other Christians. The better you are with people, the stronger your church is going to be, and the more effective it's going to be for the kingdom of God. If you're more effective at dealing with offense, and if you understand how to keep from offending others, it naturally follows that your church will experience fewer problems because of you personally. If enough people operate this way, the church becomes less susceptible to people-related problems as a whole. Conversely, when you have a congregation full of immature people with underdeveloped people skills, you are just asking for problems.

Having served in my local church for years, it became obvious to me that many people in positions of influence lack basic skills for motivating volunteers, resolving conflict, or even relating to people on a personal level. This simply will not do. If we, as a Christian body, want to truly reach the world as effectively as we can, we have to become proficient in dealing with people. Our lack of skill with people should never be the reason why someone gets offended and leaves our local church.

As Christians, we have a higher calling in life—to be with God and to reconcile as many people to Him as we can. Part of this is to meet people where they are. Initially, a lot of people we meet are going to be selfish and rough around the edges, and that's OK. We aren't condoning this behavior; we're just tolerating it until they learn a better way (like we are right now). If you take the stance that you are only going to spend your time dealing with mature communicators, it's going to be a lonely road. We should possess the necessary skill set to connect with people regardless of where they are. Once we have influence with them, we can start using that influence to help grow them into more mature communicators and Christians.

Unbelievers are constantly sizing us up. They are looking to see if we are the real deal or not. I believe being a more socially adept Christian makes you a better testimony for God. Having exceptional people skills is a great way to show people what mature Christians look like—we demonstrate our love through our words and actions. If you do the things in this book, you will be attractive to people who do not know the Lord. We want people to look at us and say, "I want what they have." They will acknowledge there is something different about you, and you will point them back to God. If we act no differently than they do, why should they accept the Lord and be born again? When we do the things outlined in this book, we are saying, "I operate on a higher level than people who don't know God." We're not all prideful about it; we just put a higher value on loving others than most unsaved people do.

One way or another, most everything in this book can be traced back to some biblical principle—God created us, He knows how we work. My intention is to add value by condensing a lot of information and going one level deeper in explaining the concepts than most of the Scriptures do. We read in the Bible about loving our neighbor; I want to give you practical examples of what that looks like in real life and how you might walk that out with *your* neighbor—even if your neighbor can be difficult most of the time.

I've divided this book into two main parts: "Laying the Foundation" and "Concrete Application." The first part is all about creating fertile soil for the other principles to grow in. Not everything in the first part is directly tied to people skills, but I believe it is necessary in order to convince you why changing is even in your best interest. It's a grab bag of life-changing principles that we'll use as a springboard into the second part of the book, which is all about giving you specific tools you can use to become more effective with others. Taken together, both parts have the ability to radically change the landscape of your life.

Part 1: Laying the Foundation

1

The HUGE Opportunity Available to Us

If you're anything like me, the first question you like to ask yourself when someone is presenting new ideas is, "Why should I even care about what you're talking about?" I would expect no less from you, the reader. After all, I already stated how opposed I am to wasting my time on things that add no value to my life, so I'm not going to do that to you. Here in the next few pages, I'm going to make it crystal clear why spending time becoming more skillful with people might be the biggest improvement you could make to your life in decades. I'm not talking about smoke and mirrors here, either. I do not believe that if we hug long enough, all of our problems will go away. Life doesn't work that way. Change comes about through deliberate decisions and perseverance.

Les Giblin, author of *Skill with People*, wrote, "Your skill with people determines the quality of your business life, your family life, and your social life." In addition, I'm going to take it a step further and say nearly every opportunity in your life is the result of a relationship with another person. "Good" relationships yield good opportunities. "Bad" relationships yield bad opportunities. How did you get your current job, meet your spouse, or even become a born-again Christian in the first place? I'm guessing it directly or indirectly came about through another person—a relationship. I was thinking about this the other day and realized that every single new employment or volunteer opportunity I've ever had was started by a connection with a person who had the influence to give me that opportunity. This includes my current position with Cradlepoint as a software developer. This is the fourth time I've worked for my current manager—she contacted me about the opportunity after she moved. If I had mismanaged my relationship with her, I wouldn't be where I am today—and I'm very happy where I'm at today.

Building and effectively managing relationships has a *huge* impact on your personal, professional, and Christian life. Speaking from personal experience, spending time developing myself in this area has resulted not only in increased happiness, which can be difficult to prove to others, but it has resulted in additional income, which is not tough to prove at all! Many organizations assess employees on leadership and communication skills, so improving yourself in these areas can have a tangible effect on your life from a financial standpoint. On at least two separate occasions when I was working for Hewlett-Packard (a technology company), my interpersonal skills put me in the next higher performance bracket, which gave me an increased pay raise and performance bonus. That's money in the bank! I'm not saying this to brag; I'm saying this to demonstrate how you can get the rewards of what we'll talk about in this book *right now*. If you serve in a local church or lead any sort of volunteer organization, putting these skills to use affects your bottom line in the form of less turnover, more engagement, and higher satisfaction in the people you're interacting with. Do not let people walk in the front door of your business or church and then walk right out the back door because you lack the necessary skills to keep them plugged in.

I recognize that most Christians are not in full-time ministry (employed by a church). Instead, they work as teachers, business owners, and electricians. The more successful you are in your career—financially prosperous and influential—the more impact you can have in this world. I want to give you some insight into ways you can become more personally successful in your career with the end result that you'll have more resources available to positively affect God's work here on the earth. I want you to be more successful at your job, and one way to do that is to become more skillful with people.

THE OPPORTUNITY TREE

The Opportunity Tree (fig. 1) is a powerful concept that has the potential to radically change your life. The "Y" circle at the bottom represents you, and all of the "P" circles are the connections you have with other people. It is greatly oversimplified, but it shows an example of the people you have a direct connection to, and then the people they have a connection to, and so on. The "O" stars are opportunities available to you through a specific relationship. These can be any kinds of opportunities: a spouse, a job, a business deal, or the ability to minister to someone. "First-tier" relationships are people you personally know (friends, family, and acquaintances), and "second-tier" relationships are friends-of-a-friend connections. The process repeats far beyond the third tier but is capped there for practical reasons.

The little fire and the box around the "branch" on the right demonstrate what happens when you mismanage a relationship with a person—when you "torch" the relationship. Not only do you miss any opportunities available through that person, such as missed business deals or influence in that person's life, you also miss any opportunities available through people whom that person knows. You know that opportunity you really, really wanted? Well, it was farther down the branch, and now you'll never see it. Do you see how huge this is? You are effectively shutting down an entire network of people when you don't practice the skills necessary to cultivate, fix, or manage the relationship with the first-tier individual. And it doesn't stop there! Those people on the right branch also have connections to other people in your tree.

We've all seen these connections play out in our lives. Have you ever asked for a recommendation concerning someone who does a particular type of work and gotten feedback like, "I heard bad things about that person"? This is the Opportunity Tree in full effect. Somewhere along the line, that individual (the worker) had a negative interaction with someone else, and you're hearing about it. This type of stuff kills all sorts of opportunities in our lives. What's even worse is many times we don't even know it's happening!

What else does the Opportunity Tree show us? It shows us that if

People Skills for Christians

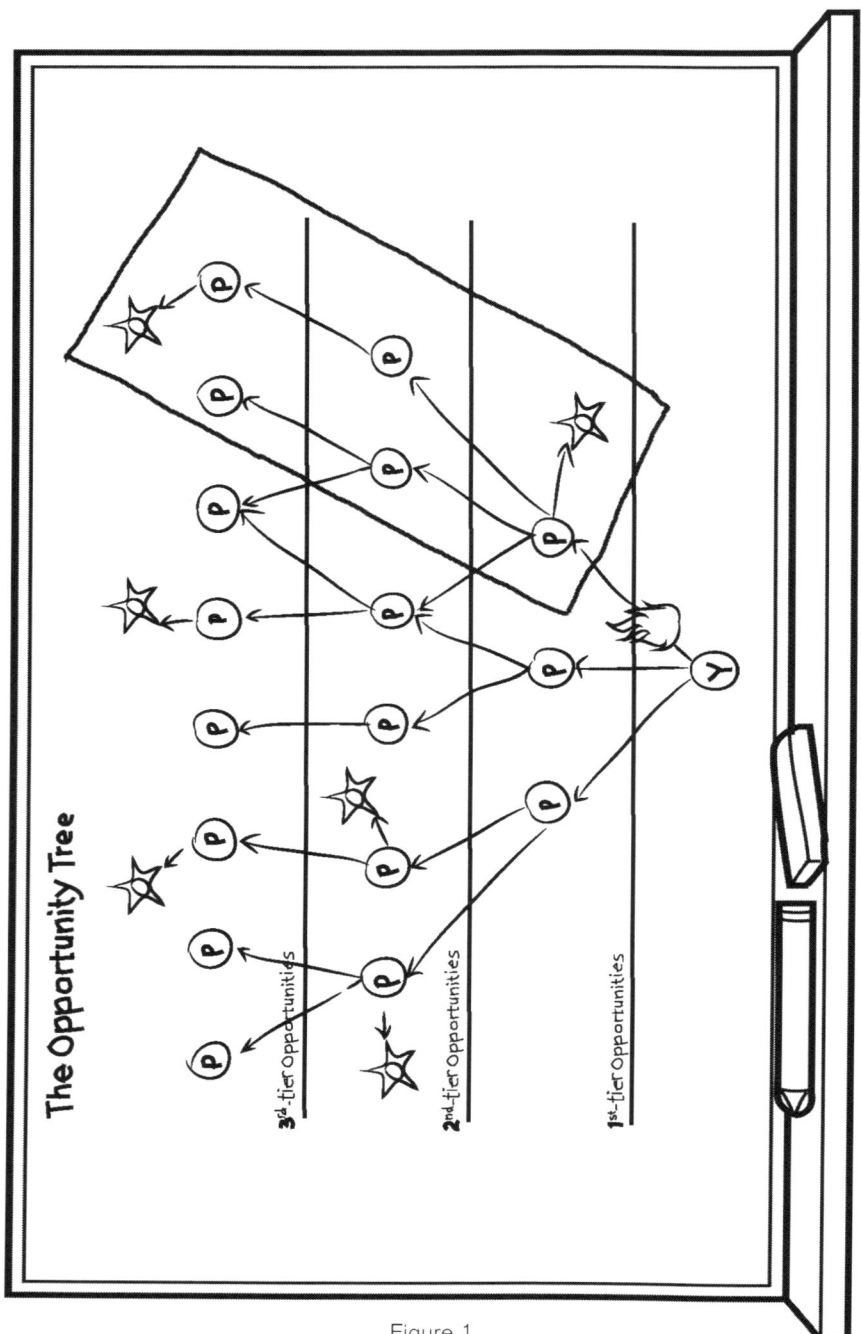

Figure 1

we want *more* opportunities—maybe a potential spouse—we need to build out our tree by adding more branches to it. This is completely under our control, and we can proactively build out our tree as full as we want it. It does depend on one thing, though: that we possess the necessary skills to add healthy relationships as new limbs. If you don't feel like you have the opportunities that other people have, you might want to look at your tree. Do you have too few branches? Do you have any healthy branches at all? If not, this could be the source of your problems—not only from a financial standpoint but from a happiness standpoint, as well. You might not need more knowledge specific to your career; you might need more healthy relationships to unlock all of those second- and third-tier connections and opportunities.

Don't just try to protect your current tree—proactively build out a bigger one! It's important to make sure your current connections with people are healthy, but focusing only on existing relationships will limit the overall size of your tree. Every chance you get, use your newfound abilities to proactively add entire new branches to your tree and watch the opportunities in your life go through the roof!

If you're like some people, you might get a little nervous when I talk about the Opportunity Tree because you don't consider yourself to be a people person. The thought of having to build out this big tree with lots of people in it might seem disturbing enough to make you want to give up before you even start. It's true that you will need to stretch yourself a little to grow your tree effectively, but I'm not going to leave you hanging here. Throughout the rest of the book, I'm going to give you tools to help you reach more people. If you're a bad conversationalist, I have some tips for you. If you have trouble meeting people, I have some ideas for that, too. Just decide that having a big tree—and all of the opportunities that come with it—is worth pursuing. I'm guessing that you had to work for most of the great things in your life. This is no different.

OUR POTENTIAL PIE

In Dale Carnegie's book *How to Win Friends and Influence People*, he stated that only 15 percent of a person's financial success is due to technical knowledge and about 85 percent is due to interpersonal and leadership skills. These statistics were based on *A Study of Engineering Education* by Charles Riborg Mann, which was published in 1918. You might be thinking to yourself: "In 1918? That's a long time ago." Yes, that's almost 100 years ago, but a recent Hay Group survey of 450 human resource directors confirmed what Carnegie wrote almost eighty years ago: Social skills are *really* important to success on the job and are looked for in potential employees. They are equally important to our overall success in life. In this book, I'll be quoting from the book of Proverbs, which is stuffed full of completely relevant wisdom and was written two to three *thousand* years ago. Human nature hasn't changed very much (if at all) in the past few thousand years, and we'll use that fact in later chapters to become better people influencers.

Another work in this space is *Emotional Intelligence* by Daniel Goleman. In his book, he talked about the importance of "emotional intelligence," which is the ability to empathize with others, regulate one's moods, and motivate oneself in the face of frustrations (among many other traits). He stated that IQ contributes, at most, 20 percent to a person's overall success in life. The other 80 percent is due to factors like one's skill with people. This means that regardless of your intelligence, the majority of your success lies in your ability to effectively manage yourself and those around you.

Realize we aren't just talking about your overall success in terms of your current situation, either. We also are talking about your overall success throughout your *entire* life. The opportunities available to you five, ten, and twenty years down the road are dependent on how skillful you are with people today. If you're thinking only within the context of your current position, that's thinking too small—think about where you want to be ten years from now, and then you'll quickly start to realize the importance of navigating relationships.

People in technical fields like engineering often don't want to believe their interpersonal and leadership skills are that important to their success. I believed the same thing for a long time, until I received a revelation of how wrong I was. It's *very* easy as humans to think our understanding of the world is how the world really works when, in reality, we might be completely wrong—but we don't think so. It's more like we've *decided* how the world works, and then we pour all of our effort into trying to excel at the game we've created. Yes, it's important to have strong skills at your job, but there is a ceiling on how far you can go with just technical ability.

Just like technical workers, it also can be tempting for Christians to put too much emphasis on knowledge. Don't get me wrong, having a solid understanding of the Bible is important, but there is a limit on how far knowledge can take you. At some point, you have to put the Bible down and go interact with people, if you want to walk in the fullness of God's calling on your life. This is when your lack of skill with people is going to start impacting your effectiveness. If you don't believe me, ask any pastor of a local church how much time he spends on issues directly related to people. You might be shocked to find out that much of his time is spent on leading and encouraging others—*not* just buried in material increasing his knowledge of biblical subjects.

For those of you who have reached great levels of success based solely on your knowledge, I challenge you with this: Just think how successful you could be if you also mastered the people skills I present in this book. Is it possible that we think we are successful, but we haven't even scratched the surface of our potential—potential only reached by being skillful with people? Remember, we aren't aware of the opportunities that pass us by when we mismanage a relationship; they just never materialize. To reach the highest levels of success in our lives, we need to be good at both: skill at our jobs and skill with people.

Figures 2 and 3 represent what I'm calling our potential and reality pies. Figure 2 represents what our total financial potential looks like, and figure 3 represents where many people probably are right now within that potential. Both are based on the 15/85 concept in Carnegie's book. I realize that some people have developed themselves more and are thus using more of their potential. The exact breakdown in figure 3 isn't important, the concept is.

Looking at figure 2, the 15 percent represents the total financial potential available to you through your technical knowledge. This would include things like how much you know about your particular area of employment and your ability to do your job.

The 85 percent represents things like your character, likability, ability

People Skills for Christians

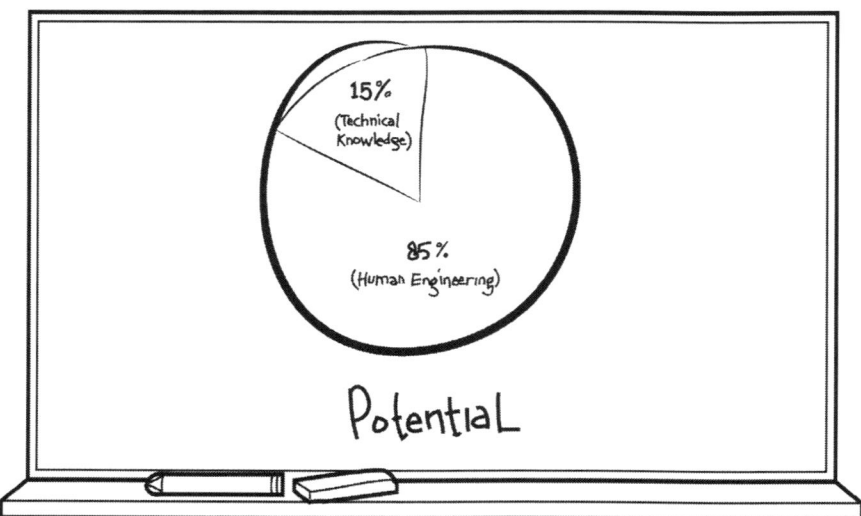

Figure 2

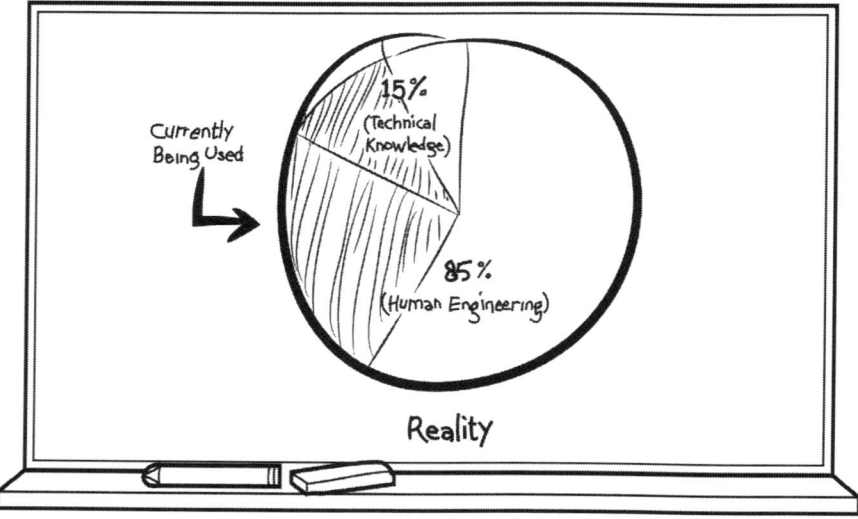

Figure 3

to forge strong relationships with people around you, and leadership ability. It basically represents everything else not associated with your raw technical know-how. This 85 percent also represents all of the opportunities available to you by proactively building out your Opportunity Tree and becoming a better leader.

Let's say you want to start your own company (or church). Your ability to attract and keep the best people is going to be heavily dependent on your skill with people—not just on your vision for the organization. Let's say someone else is starting a company, and it would be a great opportunity for you. If you mismanaged the relationships in your life, you may never get that opportunity—people won't want to work with you. This stuff happens all the time! People want to be around people they like. If you are more likable, you get more opportunities—it's just the way the world works.

I have personally been in meetings where we've discussed candidates for open positions in the company. It is *very* common for someone to speak up and say something like, "That person would be a bad fit for the company—I've worked with him before, and he has a very abrasive personality." Yup, it's the Opportunity Tree again. The person missed an opportunity because he mismanaged a relationship somewhere along the line. This is happening behind the scenes everywhere: Decisions are being made about your future, and you don't even know they are happening. Getting better at the 85 percent will help with this type of stuff.

Figure 3 is where the aha moment occurs. It's a representation of where a lot of people are in their overall potential (based on personal experience and the experiences of people I train). Out of the 15 percent of total financial potential available through technical knowledge, people seem to have harnessed most of that "slice," which is represented by the shaded part of the original 15 percent. They know how to get work done, and they know how to deliver it on time. However, if you look at the remaining 85 percent of their potential, they are not nearly as successful. I've been working on that 85 percent for years now, and I don't think I'm even close to maximizing it—not by a long shot. I suspect you're in the same boat. This diagram is important because it allows us to determine where our highest return on investment (ROI) is.

If you're like me, you may have spent years and years trying to maximize the 15 percent of your potential pie. As a software developer, there are dozens of technical books available on just the few technologies I use on a daily basis. I would keep reading books, taking courses, and practicing concepts in my free time, only to slowly climb the corporate ladder (or to stay put most of the time). It was very discouraging, too, because I was constantly surrounded by people who seemed to be better than me—they had more of a natural knack for the work. So what did I do? I kept reading more, taking more classes, and spending more and more of my time trying to maximize the 15 percent. It was exhausting, and I wasn't making the progress I was after.

I've played guitar for more than twenty years. I have practiced so much that in order for me to get better, I literally have to practice for hours and hours on whatever small, new concept it is that I'm trying to learn. Why is that? It's because I've almost maxed out my ability. There are no more huge gains to be had. I'm experiencing what is referred to as the Law of Diminishing Returns: the tendency for a continuing application of effort or skill toward a particular project or goal to decline in effectiveness after a certain level of result has been achieved. People experience the exact same thing from a career standpoint. They dump in huge amounts of time and effort trying to maximize an area with very little return available. This is why that remaining 85 percent is so important.

To fully maximize your financial potential, you have to ask yourself the question, "Where is my highest ROI?" Is it in your ability to do your work better? It might be initially, as no one can be completely incompetent and remain employed for long (though some may disagree, based on experiences with interesting individuals). OK, let's say you focus on the 15 percent. How long are you going to spend discovering that potential, and what are your plans for after it's maxed out? You eventually will hit a wall, and you'll only have one place to go for any significant gains: the other 85 percent. You *can* open up more potential by changing careers, going back to school, or starting a business, but I can guarantee that you eventually will run into the same problem again—the Law of Diminishing Returns says so.

Instead of focusing all of our time on the 15 percent, why don't we use our newfound knowledge to more quickly maximize our *overall* potential and work on *both* parts of the pie at the same time? Where is your highest ROI? If your reality pie looks more like figure 3, you have a huge amount of quick potential available to you by redirecting your energies to increasing your skill with people. You don't have to completely neglect your technical skills, but you'll need to make a shift in how you spend some of your time and energy. Many people feel like they've hit a ceiling at work, and this is the reason—there is no place left to go from a personal-efficiency standpoint. It's time to change how you play the game.

What does this look like in practice? For starters, you'll need to do things that gain you more of the 85 percent of the pie. For example, if you don't currently have a mentor, you should make it a priority to find someone who's personally more successful than you to link up with. This serves two purposes: (1) It builds out your Opportunity Tree; and (2) It connects you with someone you can learn from. You also could mentor someone yourself as a way of giving back to your organization. Company leadership loves this kind of stuff because most people don't do it. You get the benefit of helping to steer the career (and possibly life) of someone else and show your leadership team that you're not just an average employee. Another example is to join a local club in a subject you are interested in. This will instantly add more branches to your tree and get you connected with people who may hold the keys to some really great opportunities for you later down the road. Focus on what will create healthy connections and help people.

PEOPLE ARE THE GATEKEEPERS OF OUR OPPORTUNITIES

I'm from the "Nintendo Generation." I grew up playing video games, and one analogy that seems to make sense to me when talking about opportunities is the "boss" analogy. I'm not talking about *your* boss at work; I'm talking about how early Nintendo games always seemed to have some sort of boss monster at the end of a level that you'd have to defeat to go on to the next level of the game. Life is sort of this way. There is a boss who must be "defeated" to unlock that next great opportunity in your life. This doesn't happen by force; instead, we must become more skillful with people, so the gatekeeper of that great opportunity will say, "Yes, you can have my business." Or, "Yes, let's give her a promotion."

In general, people will not want to give you opportunities if they don't like you—even if you're technically qualified (possess all of the necessary skills). People want to work with other people they like. Customers want to do business with companies that treat them right. If we are abrasive individuals who create problems (of any size) wherever we go, we are automatically exempting ourselves from many great opportunities. Think about it. Would *you* promote someone into management at your company if you knew that person had a track record for creating conflict in your organization? If so, we have other problems that need to be addressed. Most leaders would never do that because they realize how many problems that can cause.

I was talking with my pastor a few weeks back about this very subject. We were talking about how, even if God was dealing with a person in a position of leadership to give an individual an opportunity, that individual's lack of skill with people would make it harder to follow God's leading. It's difficult for a leader to say to himself, "Sure, John is really poor with people, but let's put him in charge of this ministry at the church." To be honest, it's probably not going to happen.

It's critically important that we understand the concepts in this chapter. Better people skills means more healthy relationships. More healthy relationships means better opportunities for everyone involved. People skills truly are foundational life skills that all of us need to possess if we want to achieve the highest levels of success within God's plan for our lives.

2

You and God Are a Team

God works through people to get things done. If you don't believe me, just go read the Bible for a few minutes. The Bible is filled with stories of God using ordinary men and women, sometimes very flawed men and women, to get His will done on the earth. "Indeed, the Sovereign Lord never does anything until He reveals His plans to His servants the prophets" (Amos 3:7, NLT). The more you understand the plans and will of God, and the better and more skilled you are as a Christian, the more ways God can work through you.

Think about it. If you don't know something, how can you use it to affect positive change in your life or the lives of people around you? That wouldn't make sense. If you don't know what the good news is and how to lead someone in a prayer of salvation, how are you going to do it? You first need to know Jesus yourself before you can share the truth about Him or lead someone else to Him. Everyone understands this from a workplace perspective. Are you going to do the job of an electrical engineer, even though you don't know the first thing about electricity? Are you going to take over shipping responsibilities for millions of dollars' worth of merchandise leaving your company's warehouses, even though you don't know the first thing about how the shipping department operates? Of course not! You won't because you can't—you don't possess the skills for your employer to call upon.

The same goes for the promises of God. If you're unaware of what

God said concerning a particular issue, how are you going to have the faith to bring it to pass in your life? Not even Jesus could do that! "Most assuredly, I say to you, the Son can do nothing of Himself, but what He sees the Father do; for whatever He does, the Son also does in like manner" (John 5:19, NKJV). Just like Jesus, you and God are a team.

Many people believe that "God is just going to do what He's going to do"—which isn't supported by the Bible. In Romans 12:2 (NKJV), the apostle Paul said, "And do not be conformed to this world, but be transformed by the renewing of your mind, that you may prove what is that good and acceptable and perfect will of God." What's God saying here? He's saying that *you* need to change the way *you* think, so that His will can be manifest in your life. How do you do that? *You* need to get plugged in to a thriving local church where you can sit under anointed teaching, and *you* need to read God's Word so you can know how God thinks (a.k.a. renew your mind). You personally have a part to play in how far you take your Christian walk.

Another example of this can be seen in the book of Joshua. The Lord said to Joshua (in Joshua 1:8–9, NKJV): "This Book of the Law shall not depart from your mouth, but you shall meditate in it day and night, that you may observe to do according to all that is written in it. For then you will make your way prosperous, and then you will have good success. Have I not commanded you? Be strong and of good courage; do not be afraid, nor be dismayed, for the Lord your God is with you wherever you go." It was the Lord's will for Joshua to be prosperous and successful, but Joshua had a part to play in whether that would come to pass. The Lord exhorted Joshua three times in this chapter to be strong and courageous—to have faith that God was with him, causing His will to come to pass as he went—so they could work together as a team to accomplish God's plan.

In Hebrews 6:11–12 (NKJV), the author wrote, "And we desire that each one of you show the same diligence to the full assurance of hope until the end, that you do not become sluggish, but imitate those who through faith and patience inherit the promises." In these verses, we are given three requirements necessary on our part to inherit the promises of God: be active (the opposite of sluggish), and have faith and patience. All three are things *we* are accountable for, not God. The degree to which we do them is the degree to which we'll experience God in our lives. God always does His part. When we do our part, that's when the real fun begins!

If we believe God does whatever He wants, and we have no part to play, we may as well stop going to church, praying, or trying to reach the lost. It's a waste of time. We should start spending Sundays going fishing and watching more football. Throw our Bibles out the window. If God independently moves throughout the earth, we aren't going to have any effect on what He does, so why even try? It'd just be a recipe for frustration. Sounds pretty foolish, right? Don't fall into this trap, and it is a trap. We have been given specific instructions about how to get results with God—learn them and follow them. If we aren't getting the results we're promised, the problem might be that we aren't doing our part right. As Christians, we never want to water down the Word of God to suit our lack of results.

Peter talked about this in 2 Peter 1 (NKJV). Beginning in the third verse, he said that "through the knowledge of Him" we've been given "exceedingly great and precious promises." He then instructed us on how we should conduct ourselves as Christians. He told us to focus on things like diligence, virtue, knowledge, self-control, kindness, and love. He reminded us that "if you do these things you will never stumble." In other words, *you* have a part to play in experiencing more of God's will in your life.

There are numerous examples like this throughout Scripture. God is always giving us pointers on how to avoid problems in our lives. Increasing our knowledge of subjects like we'll cover in this book is important because we'll be growing in knowledge and adding more self-control, kindness, and love to our tool belts—all things Peter touched on in order to keep us from stumbling. The better you are with people, the less people problems you're going to have. The less people problems you have, the better your life is. The better you are with people, the more effective you are as a leader. There's really no downside here. The sharper the tool you are, the more useful you are to God. He still loves you, and you may be saved and going to heaven; but the more skills you have, the more uses there are for you. Increase your skill set!

If you're a sports fan, there are dozens of analogies that are applicable here. My wife really likes college basketball, and she loves watching players who can play anywhere on the court. Players who can play under the basket, dribble effectively, and shoot long-range jumpers are much more of a "threat" to the other team. They are harder to guard, and they also can fill in at other positions if you need them to. If you are a player with a single skill (you have one thing you do really well), all the other team needs to do is figure out how to shut down that one skill, and you become drastically less effective in the game. Same goes for your Christian walk. The more you know of God's Word and the more you apply that knowledge, the more of an asset you are to God—He can move you into different positions to help the team. People skills are another skill set you can develop in order to contribute to the team and be more effective.

God needs you to be more skilled at getting along with the rest of His people. We are born-again Christians and will someday be with God for eternity, but we are not there, yet. If you are reading this, it means you're still on Earth and have to contend with all of the problems on this planet. Everything we do involves people—our work, families, social lives, and churches. If we become more skilled with people, we can be more helpful to people around us and also keep from stirring up a bunch of trouble for ourselves.

I like to compare life to playing a game. Let's say you're beginning to pick up the game of chess. If you're like most newcomers, you're probably very bad at first. You make dumb moves, don't understand the strategy, and most likely lose (very quickly) to the other player, especially an experienced one. What do you do if you find yourself struggling? Do you blame the game of chess? Sadly, some people do that. In reality, however, the problem isn't with the game; the problem is that you're bad *at* the game. If you really wanted to get better, you might go take lessons, buy some books about chess, or go find a mentor to help you play the game better. The same goes for the "game of life." We might not be very good at it, yet. We need to get better at life—and we can do that!

Increasing your people skills is one surefire way to get better at the game; and in many cases, you can see positive results immediately. The better you are with people, the better your life is going to be. Period. From a Christian perspective, having strong people skills enables you to be more effective at reaching the lost and less likely to drive someone out of your local church because of saying and doing things that offend others.

God already has done His part by giving us His Word, making us right with Him through receiving Jesus, and giving us the Holy Spirit to guide us. The extent to which we use those tools is up to us. We can absolutely never read the Bible, never grow in our understanding of God, and never seek any guidance from Him. If we do that, we won't get the results we're after. However, if we take ownership of our Christian walk and grow ourselves to the best of our ability (with God's help), we will become more useful to the kingdom. As you become a better tool for God, you will unlock many of those higher-tier opportunities He has planned for you. You have a part to play in whether those opportunities will come to pass, because you and God are a team.

3

How We Get Results

Have you ever stopped to think about why your life is the way it is—why you are getting the results you are? For years, I never gave a second thought to where I was and how I got there. I robotically lived my day doing the same things I did the day before and never gave any thought to what I was doing and how that might impact where I'd be the next year. Only after I started growing in my knowledge of God, leadership, and people skills did I start putting more thought into the long-term effect my current actions were having on my life. Because of this shift in my thinking, I came up with, in the simplest terms possible, a basic formula for how we get results in our lives.

Think of figure 4 as a logical series of ordered steps people have to go through to get results (good or bad) in their lives. We start out at the top and then continue down through each step until we eventually get the results from the steps we took. The formula is simple, yet profound; and for many people, it will help them to understand where things are going wrong in their lives.

An analogy of this is the preparation of a cake. A baker sees a desirable design, thinks about how to create it, bakes and frosts it, and ends up with a cake. If the cake doesn't look like it was supposed to, it's because one of the steps was done incorrectly. The same goes for your life. If your "cake" doesn't look like you expected, it's because one of the steps was not done the correct way to get the result you were after.

You can try to fix your cake by hacking off the bad parts, pretending like it's supposed to look that way, or by putting on lots of decorations; but in the end, your cake still does not look the way it's supposed to. Even if your cake does end up looking good, it still might taste bad on the inside if the correct ingredients were not used. To consistently produce desirable results in our lives, we need to train ourselves to pay attention to the steps that lead to the results we ultimately want.

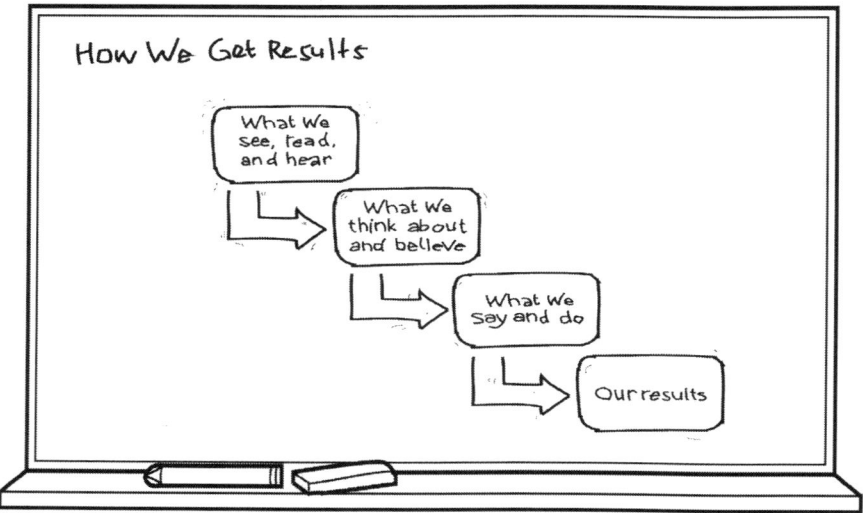

Figure 4

WHAT WE SEE, READ, AND HEAR

The first step in the formula has to do with what we're allowing into our minds—what we're "feeding" on. In general, this is going to be sensory input from our five senses (what we see, touch, smell, hear, or taste), but I've narrowed it down to the most influential of them (with two of them kind of being the same thing): what we see, read, and hear. Can you be influenced by a smell? Certainly! It's been my experience, however, that most people don't struggle in life based on what they smell, but they do struggle with what they see and hear.

Being the first step in how we get results, it's necessary that we understand its importance. We can short-circuit a whole lot of problems in life by putting some checks in place to keep us from feeding on stuff we shouldn't. If we stop things at this stage, we save ourselves from all of the related problems later down the line. The earlier we catch problems, the easier they are to correct.

I'm a software developer by trade. One thing I learned early on is how much it costs to fix a software defect based on the phase it is caught in. For example, if the developer responsible for introducing a defect into the system catches it before it's submitted, the cost to fix it is almost negligible—it never got into the system. If the defect is found by testers, it becomes more expensive because now we've used testing time to find the defect and testing resources that could have been used elsewhere. If the defect makes it to the customers, the cost of fixing it can be astronomical. If the defect is bad enough, we might lose their business. At the very least, we've now pulled in support personnel, managers, and probably more developers. The later we try to fix a problem, the more expensive it becomes. This same principle applies to our lives.

Controlling what you see is one of the primary ways to keep unhealthy content out of your mind. If you are a male living in a developed country, you know what I'm talking about here—you are constantly under attack from every sort of visual media. You can't seem to go anywhere without seeing pictures of half-naked women on magazine covers or television ads. The Internet is completely laden with pornography, so much so that it's nearly unavoidable. If you don't watch out, this can ensnare you and start you down a path toward much larger problems. Marriages end over pornography. Being a man myself, I understand what it's like to constantly be tempted. If you struggle in this area, get help! It's more common than you may think, and there are resources and people out there who can lend a hand to help you get back on track.

Women have to contend with controlling what they look at, too. There is an epidemic in America of women who think they have to be pencil thin to be attractive. Where do they get this from? Magazines, music videos, and movies constantly assault women with images of underweight models wearing size 0 dresses. If you constantly surround yourself with these sorts of images, you start to think that you're not good enough and in order to be attractive, you have to be unhealthy. Here's one easy way to avoid this: Stop feeding on those images. If you have to, cancel your subscriptions and choose to seek out information on what "healthy" actually is—bring some balance to what you're feeding on.

Over the past few years, I've run into more and more people who have begun to control what they feed on by doing things like canceling their cable TV subscriptions. Like myself, they found they were spending hours a day watching news that only seemed to report on the doom and gloom happening all over the world. It was affecting our overall happiness. Why? Because you can't consistently feed on negativity and not have it affect you. With all the options available to us today, it's entirely possible to be informed of relevant news without giving place to what others deem newsworthy, which seems to only be "news" designed to invoke fear and worry.

If something is bad for you, and you know it's bad, stay as far away from it as possible. If you don't want to have physical relations with someone you're not married to, don't put yourself in a situation where that's an option. Do what Joseph did (in Genesis 39:12) when he was tempted in this way—run! Yes, he literally ran away from the temptation. He understood that if he stayed around it long enough, he probably would give in. If you have a weight problem and want to eat healthier, don't fill your house with junk food. It's a lot easier to drive past the grocery store than to walk past the cookie aisle. If the news is affecting you in a negative way, turn it off! For me, and many others, that meant disconnecting cable.

Paying attention to what you read is another one of the primary ways to keep garbage out of your mind on the front end. You cannot consistently read ungodly material and not have it affect you. What kinds of books do you read? What kinds of articles do you seek out on the Internet? I'm not going to tell you what you should or shouldn't read, but I will tell you that what you read has an effect on your life, because that's one of the only ways material can eventually get into your thought life. If it gets into your thought life, there is a higher probability that you'll eventually act on it. If you feel like you've been reading material you shouldn't, God may be encouraging you to stop because He loves you and wants to help you avoid later problems that may result from what you've been reading.

The last way we allow things into our minds is by what we hear. This includes things like music, audiobooks, sermons or teachings, and people. Paul said (in Romans 10:17, NKJV), "So then faith comes by hearing, and hearing by the Word of God." Did you know that you can actually build up the wrong kind of faith by hearing the wrong kinds of things? Hearing the wrong things can build up your unbelief and fear, which are the total opposite of God's kind of faith. You can get so built up with unbelief and fear that it can wreck your effectiveness as a Christian. Jesus said (in Matthew 21:22, NKJV), "And whatever things you ask in prayer, *believing*, you will receive" (italics added for emphasis). Unbelief will destroy your prayer life. One way to give your Christian walk a shot in the arm is by listening to material that is in line with God's Word. This will build the right kind of faith in your life—and then when you do pray, you'll get better results.

Whatever you "feed" becomes stronger, and whatever you "starve" gets weaker. If you are constantly feeding on material that promotes fear, anxiety, and depression, those kinds of emotions will grow stronger in you. If you constantly view inappropriate material on the Internet, the desire for that material will grow. Conversely, though, if you feed on things like God's Word and anointed biblical teaching, those desires also will grow stronger in you. Pick what you want to grow inside of you and feed it with the right kinds of food.

If you are currently in an undesirable place because of what you've been watching, reading, or hearing, my advice for you is this: Starve it! Start feeding the other parts of you that you want to grow. It won't be easy at first, but it *will* get better. Trade news time for Bible time. Trade your ungodly reading material for an online teaching from your favorite pastor. If something is *really* hard to resist, do what Joseph did: Remove yourself from the situation. Do whatever you have to—pull the life support on what is producing bad results in your life.

WHAT WE THINK ABOUT AND BELIEVE

The next step to getting results in our lives (either good or bad) is what we think about and believe. I will talk about the thought life in depth in a later chapter, but I want to give you a little teaser now, as it fits in with the formula we are discussing. Introducing all of the stages of the formula now, before we continue with the rest of the book, will give you a better understanding of where later concepts fit in.

After we've seen, read, or heard something (the first step in the formula), we now have the *choice* to think about the information that has come in. Realize that we do have a choice in what we think about. My pastor has a saying that goes something like this: You can't keep a bird from flying over your head, but you can keep it from making a nest in your hair. We can't always control what we see or hear, but we can decide if we want to think about it—that choice is completely up to us. Realize that if we do think about something, we now are one step closer to seeing the results from those thoughts in our lives. Be very careful! For good or bad, you are now one step closer to getting the results from what you've been feeding on. If someone tells you that God wants you sick, broke, and depressed, and you allow yourself to think about it long enough, you run the risk of believing it. If you believe it, you will act that way (the third part of the formula), and you will get sick, broke, and depressed results. See how powerful this is? Incorrect thoughts bring about incorrect results.

I heard someone say that there should be a "bouncer" at the door of each Christian's thought life. If something comes in that is contrary to what God says, the bouncer kicks it out. This bouncer is you! You can, without a doubt, control your thought life. If you don't believe you can, you are being deceived. In 2 Corinthians 10:5 (NKJV), Paul talked about how "bringing every thought into captivity to the obedience of Christ" is a major part of our personal spiritual warfare. If we want to succeed in life and follow God's plan for our lives to the fullest, we need to control our thoughts. If something comes into your head, and you don't want to think about it—don't. Kick it out!

It's been my observation that people want to read, watch, and think about whatever they want to, but then they expect to get results like they've been in God's Word all day long renewing their minds to who they are in Christ. Acting this way is very similar to having unprotected sex with your spouse and really, really hoping a pregnancy doesn't occur. That is a dangerous way to live if you don't want to have children, yet—you're basically rolling the dice each and every time you participate in that behavior. People are doing the same thing with their thought lives. They are feeding on ungodly information, thinking about ungodly information, and then crossing their fingers and hoping it all just works out in their favor in the end. Control what you let in, and control what you think about!

If your thought life is out of control, realize you are not powerless. You can stop bad thoughts in their tracks. It might take a little work at first, but what other option do you have? If I'm speaking to you, I recommend you find out what God says about your situation and start repeating that to yourself. One Scripture you can use is 2 Timothy 1:7 (NKJV): "For God has not given us a spirit of fear, but of power and of love and of a sound mind." If you are a born-again Christian, you have a sound mind. Get in agreement with what God says about you and watch your life start to change.

WHAT WE SAY AND DO

The third step in the formula is what we say and do. It's where the rubber meets the road, and we take what we've fed on and what we've been thinking about and turn it into a physical reality in our lives. There are only two ways we get things done in life: influencing through speech or physically doing something. This step is our last opportunity to control ourselves before we get results, so it's very important that we act intentionally both in speech and in action. All of our hard work changing our habits and thoughts can be for nothing if we don't control our mouths (there's a whole chapter on this later) or don't follow through with the correct physical actions (there's also an entire chapter later on the power of "do"). Sadly, this is the step where many people fail when trying to get positive results in their lives—they don't do the necessary actions to bring about the change they are looking for.

Many studied Christians have come short of God's plan for their lives because they haven't taken God's Word from the pages of the Bible and acted on it in faith. Faith is what activates God's Word and is almost always demonstrated with some sort of physical response, such as a confession with our mouths, at least initially. In Mark 11:23 (NKJV), Jesus said, "For assuredly, I say to you, whoever says to this mountain, 'Be removed and be cast into the sea,' and does not doubt in his heart, but believes that those things he says will be done, he will have whatever he says." That's three times in one verse Jesus told us to speak what we believe. He didn't tell us to pray in our thoughts or think about what we wanted, He instructed us to speak. You'll also notice that He didn't say to pray to God *about* the mountain, either—He told us to speak to the mountain ourselves. Do not underestimate the power of your words!

Following up our thoughts with actions is what creates the tangible (physical) from the intangible (thoughts). The only way we are going to see results in our lives is by converting our intangible thought life into physical activity that can produce results. No amount of wishing or hoping will take the place of physically doing whatever activity produces the desired result in our lives. Do you want to see more people being led to the Lord? Well, go *do* it! Have you always wanted to start your own business? Well, I guarantee you it will *never* happen if you don't get to the point where you physically do the actions necessary to start it and make it successful.

The difference between ourselves and others whom we deem more successful is they are simply doing the correct actions to be successful. They have fed on material that has changed how they think, established healthy habits, and then took the next step and started doing something with that knowledge. They probably aren't any smarter than us; they just *do* what is necessary to be successful. They have gotten over their fear and realized the only way they're going to see results appear in their lives is by following up their thoughts with actions. If we started doing the right things, we'd start seeing the right results, too.

In my opinion, the do stage is where a lot of people try to "hold it all together." They feed on the wrong things (step 1), think about the wrong things (step 2), and then desperately try to get good results by forcing themselves to do the right thing. And we wonder why we are unhappy! Constantly thinking one way and not being able to act it out is a recipe for torment. Think about it for a minute. If you're a woman who constantly watches movies and reads romance novels in which the men are unrealistically romantic and passionate, and your real-life husband is not, that is going to produce an unfulfilled desire inside of you. You want your husband to be like a fictional character and may even voice that to him. Best case is he'll change. In reality, he probably won't, and it will be a source of dissatisfaction for you. See how this works? Feeding on unhealthy material, in whatever form, can have real, negative effects on your physical life. The same principle works in other ways, too.

OUR RESULTS

Finally, this is where—for good or bad—we're going to get the results of the previous three steps we've taken up to this point. If we've fed on the right stuff, thought about the right stuff, and done the right stuff, we're going to get good results. If we've allowed ourselves to feed and think on garbage and also acted on that garbage, we are going to get bad results. It's literally no more complicated than that.

Do not be deceived as to why you are not getting the results you want in your life. We get exactly what we have been working toward. If this challenges you, don't be condemned—be encouraged! What this means is you have the ability to get your life back on track (with God's help) and get the results you're after. Find the step where you're off and go back and fix it!

In Matthew 19:26 (NKJV), Jesus said that "with God all things are possible." He also said (in Mark 9:23, NKJV), "If you can believe, all things are possible to him who believes." You have bright days ahead with God on your side, regardless of where you've come from or where you are right now.

As I close this chapter, I want to encourage you to apply the formula we just went over to your life. Don't just think about it—*do* something with it. Ask yourself, "What do I feed on every day?" If you find that you are feeding on and thinking on the right stuff but not getting the results you want, consider how to change what you are saying and doing in step 3. If you start doing the good stuff you already are thinking about, you *will* get the results from that—that's just how it works. Don't stop short of the do phase! Follow through with what you know to be right and true, so you can see the effects of it manifest in your life.

4

Your Thought Life Determines Your Reality

We touched on this a little in the previous chapter, but it's a big enough topic that it warrants a chapter of its own. What we think about all day long is directly connected to the results we are getting in life. We cannot think about failure, defeat, and inadequacy all day and then expect to live victorious lives—it just isn't going to happen.

REPROGRAM YOUR THOUGHT LIFE

As I stated previously, what we think about is in large part influenced by what we allow ourselves to see, read, and hear. Proverbs 4:23 (NIV) says, "Above all else, guard your heart, for everything you do flows from it." Your heart, in this Scripture, is not your physical heart; it's your mind, will, and emotions. Solomon was saying: "Hey, make sure you set up a barrier between you and the rest of the world. Don't allow just anything in. Make sure it checks out with God's Word before you let it in." This is where the bouncer I talked about in the previous chapter can help out: Kick out the potential threat before it has a chance to take hold in your mind.

Stephen R. Covey, a popular self-help guru, said, "You can't change the fruit without changing the root." This is just another way of saying what Jesus said (in Matthew 12:33, NIV), "Make a tree good and its fruit will be good, or make a tree bad and its fruit will be bad, for a tree is recognized by its fruit." If we want good "fruit" in our lives, we need to make our "trees" good. How can we make our trees better? Well, for starters, we need to recognize how important our thought lives are and that we have complete control over which thoughts are allowed to stay.

We can't go anywhere in our bodies that we haven't gone first in our minds. This is an important concept to get ahold of because if we *don't* want to go somewhere in our lives (don't want bad results), then we don't want to go there in our minds first. It also means that if we *do* want to go somewhere in our lives (want good results), we *first* need to go there in our minds. Like I said previously, we can't act on information we don't know or have. We first need to get the good information in our minds, and then we can make it a physical reality in our lives.

All of the major battles in our lives are won and lost between our ears. Many people concede defeat before they've moved even a single muscle in the physical world. They've allowed the lies of this world to beat them down to the point where they don't think they can succeed at anything they do. They believe in their heart that they are failures who will never amount to anything and will never have the ability to change the circumstances around them. Says who? You? That's not what God says about you. In Romans 8:31 (NKJV), Paul (inspired by the Holy Spirit) said, "If God is for us, who can be against us?" Later in that same chapter, he called us "more than conquerors." Does that sound like the description of a failure to you? *You are not a victim!*

Many people, including myself, live in an imaginary prison of false thinking. Because of past hurts, off-handed comments by people we've come in contact with, or temporary failures, we've constructed a small, six-by-eight-foot cell for ourselves that we could occupy for the rest of our lives. "No, don't go outside the walls—it's not safe!" That kind of thinking is exactly what the enemy (Satan) wants from you. If you're born again, he has already lost the battle for your spirit (your eternal future), so the next best thing for him is to keep you ineffective inside of a prison he happily helps you create in your own mind. Don't let him do it! Jump the wall and blow the doors off of the *real* you, not the person someone else told you that you are. That's why the Bible is so valuable—it tells you who you really are. Jesus said (in John 8:32, NKJV), "And you shall know the truth, and the truth shall make you free." We need to reprogram our minds with the truth. How do we do that?

The Word of God is the primary mechanism for reprogramming our thoughts—it's the granddaddy of all self-help books. In addition to reading the Bible, it's important to find Spirit-led teachers who can help grow you. These men and women have a specific calling on their lives, placed there by God, to help you. Together with the leading of the Holy Spirit, they can quickly grow you into a mature Christian.

If you are not part of a church where God is moving, you are missing out on one of the primary ways God can grow you. My pastor has been one of the single biggest influencers in my life. He has devoted his life to studying, hearing from God, and then teaching what he's learned to the church he pastors. Finding a great pastor is kind of like finding a great mechanic when your car is having trouble. You could possibly figure out how to fix the problem yourself, but it will more than likely take you longer than you want and cost you more than you want to spend, and the results might not be as good as if you just hired someone who does it for a living. The same principle applies to reprogramming your broken mind—it's better to find a professional. What's really nice is it doesn't cost you anything—your pastor will do it for free! Go find a thriving local church and use the material in this book to start building healthy relationships!

Many problems can be completely avoided altogether by simply choosing what we give our attention to—by keeping the garbage out in the first place. Then, if we transition to only feeding on the right material, we can wholesale flush the rest of the system. An analogy my pastor has used is comparing a person's thought life to a glass of chocolate milk. If you wanted to remove the chocolate from the glass, would you try to separate the chocolate from the milk? No! Just pour more milk into the glass until it flows out, and eventually the chocolate will be gone. If your mind is full of garbage right now, it's easier to pour more of God's "milk" into you, which will force out the garbage, than it is to do anything explicitly with the garbage. All you have to do is put in the new milk. Don't focus on the bad; focus on getting more of the good. Over time, you'll notice your thought life begin to change, and it won't be through raw force of will—you let God change you from the inside out.

OUR THOUGHTS PRODUCE ACTIONS

I've mentioned this before, but I believe it's really important that we get a solid understanding of where our thoughts fit into the process of influencing the overall quality of our lives. Our actions are a byproduct of what we spend our time thinking about, so it's very important to maintain control of our thought lives. Our thoughts produce actions, which then produce the circumstances and opportunities in our lives. If we want better circumstances and opportunities, we need better thoughts.

You may have heard the saying: "If you think you can't, you're right. If you think you can, you're right." If you think you're not smart enough, you won't even attempt to do things that you believe are too difficult for you. If you think you're not attractive, you won't even approach the handsome man or woman and ask for a date. If you have not guarded your heart, you've let other people place *their* limitations on you. I may not know you personally, but I can guarantee you're achieving far less in life than you're capable of. You've let other people place barriers on you, and worst of all, you believe them! When you believe them, you act on what you believe and get the results of believing the lies. You don't think you are smart enough to go to college and graduate at the top of your class? Says who? You think you're destined to struggle for the rest of your life because the news media keep telling you how bad the economy is? Is that what God says about you? If you are a born-again Christian, God says you have the "mind of Christ" (1 Corinthians 2:16). This means you have the same mind that equipped apostles to change the world with the gospel. You have the same mind that knew how to perfectly answer the questions and accusations of the religious sect of Jesus's day. You have the Holy Spirit inside of you, teaching and directing you. You have an edge in life in everything you do; you just need to draw on it.

Our thoughts influence our decisions. Our decisions determine our direction. And our direction determines our destination. No amount of effort trying to force the right kind of results to occur in our lives is going to work like we want it to in the long run. This sort of approach to change is similar to crash dieting. You may get some results in the short term, but it's not a sustainable way to keep weight off. We'll eventually get tired of trying to manage our lives this way, and things will start to break down and return to the way they were.

Have you ever wondered why seemingly "perfect" people and families have major, unexpected meltdowns? You know, where the husband and wife all of a sudden seem to explode in a gigantic supernova of unexplainable behavior? I can guess what the problem was: They tried to hold everything together at the results phase, instead of building a strong foundation for results by properly managing their thoughts. Instead of reprogramming their thoughts and spending their days thinking like God thinks, they tried unsuccessfully to think one way and act another. It just doesn't work. Henry Cloud, a clinical psychologist, once said, "We change our behavior when the pain of staying the same becomes greater than the pain of changing." People can only live contrary to their true hearts, regardless of whether that's good or bad, for so long before they become dissatisfied and decide to align their physical actions with their thoughts (or true selves) in order to ease the pain of constantly living a lie. I'm not trying to get all analytical on you, I'm just trying to point out that you can only live in direct opposition to your thought life for so long until the real you pops its head up. If I'm describing you, do not despair! The solution is to change the real you by changing the way you think.

If you have unsatisfying relationships in your life, it's time to change how you think, so you can get better results. Maybe you don't think you're a people person. That's a lie. Maybe you think it's too hard, and you don't have the time to learn the necessary skills. That's a lie, too. Or, maybe you think it's not worth the effort. I will do my best to help change your attitude. One thing is for certain: By reading this book, you are taking a step toward increasing your quality of life—you are feeding on material that can positively impact the way you think.

5

The Power of 'Do'

It doesn't matter what you know, it matters what you do. You could have the sum total of all the information you could ever learn stored inside of your head, but if you're not doing anything with it, it's not benefiting you at all. In this chapter, I will spend some time trying to motivate you to do something with the information you have already learned—and will learn—in this book.

There are entire industries and personalities trying to get you to do something. Not all of them are bad, either. The school system tries to get kids to eat right by teaching them the food pyramid. The government tries to get people to live healthier by requiring food labels on things we buy at a grocery store. Your pastor tries to get you to put spiritual truths into practice, so you can see more of God's will manifest in your life. In a way, I guess, I'm jumping on that train, too, because I'm going to spend this chapter explaining why doing something with the information you have is the key to unlocking all of the beneficial knowledge in your head. This chapter expands on some of the ideas we talked about in chapter 3.

KNOWLEDGE IS ONLY POTENTIAL POWER

Napoleon Hill, author of *Think and Grow Rich*, said: "Knowledge is only potential power. It becomes power only when, and if, it is organized into definite plans of action, and directed to a definite end." That's a powerful statement. Many people seem to believe knowledge is power, but that isn't entirely true. It's only power *if* it's put to use. What does that mean for us? Well, for starters, not doing anything with what we know is equivalent to not knowing it. That's right—all of that great info we've talked about so far isn't going to do us any good until we decide to do something with it. It doesn't stop there, though, because this principle applies to every area of our lives. You know how to read but don't? Guess what. You're getting the same results as someone who is illiterate. You memorized the Bible but don't do anything it says? In reality, you are no better than someone who's never read the Bible at all. God still loves you, and you may be going to heaven when you die, but all of that biblical knowledge isn't doing you any good.

The key to getting results in life is to do something with what we know. Acting on our good thoughts is the bridge between our thought lives and the results we want. There's no other way to get the results we want except to act on what we currently know to do. As Christians, we don't want to be deceived into thinking that just because we know the Word of God, we are going to get the results it says we'll get. We also don't want to think that spiritual maturity is based on knowledge—it's not. The true sign of spiritual maturity is how much of God's Word we are putting into practice in our lives—how much we are doing—and the results we are getting from it.

The apostle James said the same thing (in James 2:14–26, NKJV) when he wrote that "faith without works is dead." He isn't talking about Old Testament Jewish law here, or that we have to earn our way into a relationship with God—Jesus did this for us. He's saying that our proclamation of faith by itself doesn't prove anything if it isn't accompanied by action. Many Christians seem to think that prayer will somehow get God's will done on the earth by itself. Prayer is an important component of being a Christian; but at some point, *someone* has to be the person who preaches the gospel to the lost. *Someone* has to be the person who gives to the local church. *Someone* has to be the person to go to the hospital and minister to the sick. If everyone only prayed, who would do the work? The answer is simple. Everyone should pray *and* show his or her faith with good "works" (action).

ALL OF THE POWER IS IN THE 'DO'

Many Christians appear to be in a permanent state of preparation. They live their lives as in a halftime, locker-room pep talk. They may even read their Bible every day, go to church twice a week, and pray every morning. Is there anything wrong with that? Absolutely not! But if that's where they stop, they are never going to fulfill God's purpose for their lives. At some point, they need to put the Bible down and get in the game. This same principle applies to getting better results with people.

If we want better relationships with people, we have to change the way we interact with them. There is no other way. We can't change other people; the only person you can change is yourself. If this is the only "knob" we can turn, we may as well start turning it by learning how to become more skillful with people—not just in thought but in action. Trust me, I know from personal experience that it's a complete waste of time trying to change another person by forcing them to do anything. It doesn't work. All they'll do is end up resenting you. The right way to go about it is this: Change yourself and then exert positive influence over others to bring about the change you're after.

If your wife isn't treating you right, what do you do? Do you yell at her, argue with her, and play mind games until you've forced her to do the right thing? Doesn't work. She'll just resent you. If you can't do that (can't keep doing what you've been doing), how are you supposed to fix the problem? Easy. Treat her exactly like you want her to treat you. Put the Golden Rule, which I'll talk about more later, into full effect. That's right! You're going to *do* something with that principle you learned in the first grade! Love her more. Respect her more. Show her how much you appreciate her. This is far more effective than escalating the marital arms race and forcing someone into compliance. If you're struggling in this area, that little nugget right there can change your life. It's an example of putting what you know into practice, so you can get the result you want.

If you're a devoted Christian and are not as far along as you'd like to be in your walk with God, the reason may be because you are not doing anything with the knowledge you already have. A simple fix to your stagnation may be to simply act on what you already know.

Jesus, in Matthew chapter 25 (NKJV), gave us the parable of the talents to demonstrate how God thinks. In the parable, Jesus talked about three servants and how their master gave them each "talents" (think money, but personal abilities works, too). While he was gone, each servant did different things with the talents—two invested them, and one buried it in the ground. When their master came back, each servant had to give an account of what he did with the talents. The master commended the two who had invested his talents and received an increase on their investment. He chided the third who buried his talent and did nothing with it. The master took the talent from him and gave it to the servant who earned the most on his initial amount. What does this tell us about how God thinks? It tells us that if we are diligent with what we have and multiply it, God will give us more. If we're not doing anything with the wisdom and understanding God already has given us, why would He give us more?

For many Christians, it's not a lack of the knowledge of God that's holding them back but a lack of acting on what they already know. Many Christians seem to think that if they can just hear one more teaching in a particular area, then all of a sudden (without having to do anything), everything will start working for them. That is a total lie—it'll never happen. For many of us, if we never heard another biblical teaching for the rest of our lives, we'd still have more than enough knowledge to radically change our own lives and the lives of the people around us until we die. The shortfall is not in our knowing; it's in our doing. We were warned (in James 1:22, NKJV), "But be doers of the Word, and not hearers only, deceiving yourselves."

The simplest way to increase your quality of life *right now* is to pick something you know you should be doing and just do it. If you know you're not appreciating people in your life like you should, just go do it! If you know you haven't been spending as much time with your kids as you should, start spending time with them. Just pick one thing and do it. If you're like me, it's easy to get overwhelmed with all of the stuff I should be doing. The only way to feel better about it is to unplug the dam and start draining that to-do list. There's no silver bullet. There's no magic pill. It's about recognizing the importance of following up thoughts with actions and then executing on your plan.

I cannot possibly overemphasize the importance of acting on the good information you already have. As you go through this book, pick things that resonate with you the most and start implementing them. You *will* get the results it says you'll get, if you make it part of your daily life.

I have a friend named "Steve" where I work. He's an MIT graduate. He's amazingly smart—one of the smartest people I have met. Because of his position, he needed to lead cross-functional teams and was running into some people problems. The problems were significant enough that he was referred to me, and we started meeting every week to go through much of the same material I'm covering in this book. As we started going through the information, he began having what typically are referred to as "aha moments." He saw where he was making mistakes with people, and he immediately changed his behavior—he stopped doing the things that were giving him undesirable results and started doing things a better way. What were the results of changing his actions? The situation changed almost immediately. Why was Steve successful? He was successful because he saw where he was off, learned a better way, and then implemented the better way immediately. The exact same process will work for you. It's funny, because some people are real quick to implement changes in their lives, and some people drag their feet for years. He was lightning fast in implementing the changes and saw results almost as quickly. Be like Steve!

6

People Are Predictable

I may not know you, but I bet I could tell you a lot about yourself even without ever personally meeting you. I bet you want to be loved. I bet you want to feel important and appreciated for all of the good things you do. I bet you want to make a nice living and live a comfortable life without having to worry about money problems. I also bet that you want to feel like what you're doing actually means something in the long run and that you'd like to leave some sort of positive legacy after you're gone. Did I get close? How was I able to do that? It's easy—the same desires have motivated people throughout history. To put it another way, we haven't changed much in thousands of years.

In 1 Corinthians 10:13 (NKJV), Paul said, "No temptation has overtaken you except such as is common to man." Paul told us that we all deal with the same temptations. This is because we were born with the same nature. Greed, lust, pride—the same sorts of temptations have led to the downfall of men since we were created. These temptations are used against us because they work—we are predictable.

Because people haven't changed that much, we can use that information to our advantage. I don't mean that in a manipulative, self-seeking way; I mean it in an I-know-what-I'm-dealing-with-here kind of way. Understanding the fundamental nature of people gives us a huge advantage when dealing with them because we can avoid the things they don't like and cater to the things they do. For instance, we know people like to be appreciated, so we'd be foolish not to use that knowledge to keep the people around us happy and motivated by appreciating them more. We know people like gifts, so we'd be amiss for not liberally showering them on the people around us. This is how we demonstrate that people are important to us. Anyone can say people are important, but we'll *show* people they are important to us with our actions.

PEOPLE LIKE TO BE 'OPERATED' A SPECIFIC WAY

Just like there are a series of actions you need to go through to start your car and successfully pull it out of the garage, there is a proper way to interact with people that will give you the results you are after. Violate those rules, and people won't "work" correctly. It's not their fault, either—you are the one misusing them! The more we understand about human nature, the more effective we can be at influencing people. Influence is the only way to bring about long-term change. Force or manipulation will ultimately fail.

As soon as I started understanding human nature a little better, I began applying the principles I was learning to different situations at my workplace. On one particular occasion, another member of my team and I had the unfortunate task of meeting with a group of contractors to figure out why they weren't performing a specific job as well as we'd like. I distinctly remember talking to my teammate on the way to the meeting and telling her to watch as I was about to apply some new skills I had learned. Upon entering the room, I began to apply about a half dozen principles we'll go over in this book. I started by telling the contractors how much we appreciated all of the work they did for us (they did more than just what I came to talk to them about). I communicated to them how important their work was to the overall success of the company. I then asked them if there was anything we could do to help them, or if they were having any problems. At this point, they voluntarily admitted to not meeting the bar on the specific job I was most interested in, and they even went so far as to come up with their own plan to fix it! I never said a single word about the problem area. Instead, I focused on what they were doing right and put them at ease, so they felt comfortable confronting the problem as a team. My teammate left the meeting amazed. So was I. The meeting actually strengthened our relationship with them. I suppose I could have jumped all over them, but that would have been "operating" them in the wrong way. I used my understanding of people to get the results I was after without burning any bridges with the team.

If we criticize people, they don't like it. If we tell people they are wrong, they don't like it. If we take people for granted, they don't like it. These are just three simple examples but they demonstrate what we are talking about. We can use our understanding of human nature to avoid the land mines.

Our understanding of human nature becomes even more powerful when we start to use it to get positive results. If you manage people, you understand that humans really like it when you ask them for their opinions on decisions that need to be made. I'm not saying that everyone has an equal vote in making the decision, just that people like to be asked for their opinions. People love this because they feel included in the solution. Humans also like to be told, "Good job," especially in front of other people—it's just how we are wired. We'll talk more about things like this in later chapters.

MOST PEOPLE ARE ONLY CONCERNED WITH THEMSELVES

In general, people are only concerned with themselves. They have their own set of problems, and those problems are far more important to them than anyone else's. They are primarily interested only in what makes them feel good, both physically and mentally, and will resist anything that runs contrary to that nature. Understanding that people have a predictable selfish nature, which is really just a form of immaturity, will help us influence them more effectively in the initial stages of our relationship with them. This understanding will give us a mental buffer when interacting with them. Instead of becoming offended because of someone's behavior, we can prepare ourselves for it, and then it becomes easier to overlook. If we know that people are naturally selfish, we won't be surprised when they make selfish decisions—it's human nature. For believers, it's part of our unrenewed minds. Give others some time and space to grow. Be patient with them while they mature.

A local church should *always* have people of varying degrees of maturity in it. This is a good thing because it means you're attracting the lost and keeping them around long enough to grow them into mature Christians. This is the way it should be and is a sign of a healthy church body. Because of this, a growing church always will have people in it who are selfish initially and need extra shepherding through the maturation process. If we don't know how to effectively deal with their mental and spiritual immaturity, we risk losing them and not being able to minister to them at all. I never want someone to leave my church because of my lack of skill with people. The good news is we can become much more effective at dealing with people. By practicing just a handful of foundational people skills, we can keep from offending and being offended while the immature believers come up to speed.

A quick note of caution: Just as we could assume a Christian who has been saved for many years is mature, we also could assume others are more emotionally mature than they actually are. Having unrealistic expectations can open yourself up to taking offense to something they say or do when you think they should know better. Don't look for the worst in people but use wisdom in dealing with them. Assuming people are more developed than they are can cause unnecessary heartburn on your end.

Understanding that people are generally only concerned with themselves can be valuable from a leadership standpoint, as well. In chapter 22, I'll talk about how one of the major ways to motivate people is to find out what's important to them and then use that as a "carrot" to influence them. I'm not talking about empty promises and manipulation, either. What I'm talking about is learning an individual's personal goals so you can figure out how they can align with the goals of your organization to keep the individual motivated and engaged. You get what you want, and the other person gets what he wants, too.

By understanding the predictable behavior of others, we can help each other to grow in maturity together and, in the process, strengthen our church body or organization. A strong church or workplace is built on the backs of mature individuals. If you use your knowledge of human nature to more patiently influence others, you are making a real, tangible difference. The people in charge will thank you, and the people you interact with will feel more connected than they ever have. This is how you make someplace the best place to work—through personal ownership of the relationships.

7

The Law of Sowing and Reaping

Just like there are physical laws that govern our universe, there also are spiritual laws that affect our existence while we are living on the earth. They are called spiritual laws because they originate from God and always are operating—regardless of whether we choose to believe in them or not. From a Christian standpoint, we want to be aware of these laws because when our lives are in alignment with them, we get the blessings God says we'll get when we obey them.

The law of sowing and reaping has been known by Christians and non-Christians for hundreds of years. A very simple explanation of the law goes something like this: Whatever you "sow" (give, invest into a person, say, etc.) is exactly what you will "reap" (have returned to you). The secular world may refer to it as karma or "what goes around, comes around." Yes, even the secular world has identified the concept of sowing and reaping but just doesn't give credit to God for it. Unbelievers have recognized that an intangible (spiritual) law governs our actions with each other and that people should be aware of it, so we can have more control over our future.

In Galatians 6:7–10 (TLB), Paul said: "Don't be misled; remember that you can't ignore God and get away with it: a man will always reap just the kind of crop he sows! If he sows to please his own wrong desires, he will be planting seeds of evil and he will surely reap a harvest of spiritual decay and death; but if he plants the good things of the

Spirit, he will reap the everlasting life that the Holy Spirit gives him. And let us not get tired of doing what is right, for after a while we will reap a harvest of blessing if we don't get discouraged and give up. That's why whenever we can we should always be kind to everyone, and especially to our Christian brothers." Paul explained to us how to get good results in our lives—we have to plant good seeds.

Paul, inspired by the Holy Spirit, used a farming example that anyone can understand to say, "Hey, the kingdom of God works just like this!" Isn't it interesting to consider the connection between the physical world and the spiritual realm? I guess it shouldn't be surprising, since the same person created both—God!

But wait, it gets even better! In 2 Corinthians 9:6 (NKJV), Paul said, "But this I say: He who sows sparingly will also reap sparingly, and he who sows bountifully will also reap bountifully." Paul specifically talked about financial giving in this chapter, but this exact same principle applies to sowing in other areas, as well. With regards to the relationships in our lives, if we sow little, we reap little. If we sow a lot, we reap a lot.

We'd be wise to notice that the law is *not* called reaping and sowing. Many people want to reap the benefits of making wise decisions and properly investing in people's lives before they have sown anything into those areas. It doesn't work that way. We sow first and then we reap. This means initially a lot of our sowing is going to be done in faith because we won't have anything to point to as proof that it's working. Hang in there! In due season, we *will* reap.

IF YOU DON'T WANT CORN, DON'T PLANT CORN SEEDS

Picture this scenario: A farmer goes down to the local supply store and buys a bunch of corn seeds. He comes home and, after confidently preparing the soil in his garden, starts putting his corn seeds in the ground. Purposefully, he puts the corn seeds in nice, straight rows the perfect distance apart, so each one of his plants will have just the right amount of space to flourish. After planting, he begins to water his seeds. Weeks go by, and the plants start to break through the soil and grow. Quickly, they are a few feet high. The farmer, having been gone for a couple of weeks on a much-needed vacation (do farmers actually take vacations?), walks out to his field, takes a look at his crop, and says, "Where are all my tomatoes?"

What would you tell the farmer? You'd probably tell him, "If you didn't want corn, you shouldn't have planted corn seeds."

This story may seem a little silly, but people operate this exact same way in their daily lives—they plant one kind of seed and expect to reap a different kind of crop. All day long, people plant different kinds of seeds in their gardens, not realizing that just as assuredly as planting corn seeds in a garden will produce corn plants, the seeds they plant in their lives also will produce after the types of seeds planted. This law is massive in its application because it affects so many different areas of our lives! Think about it. Think about all of the interactions we have with people. Each of these interactions is an opportunity to sow a seed into their lives.

WHAT'S IN YOUR GARDEN?

People can tell what we've planted based on what's growing in our gardens. If you had a garden in your backyard, it would take me less than one minute to tell you *exactly* what kinds of seeds you planted. You could argue with me, tell me there's no way you planted a certain kind of vegetable; but in the end, the garden speaks for itself. Corn seeds have not produced, do not produce, nor will they ever produce tomato plants. What's growing in our gardens is exactly what we've planted, whether we choose to acknowledge it or not.

If our lives are full of stress, depression, broken relationships, or alienation from everyone around us, others could tell us exactly what kinds of seeds we planted. They wouldn't have to have been there when we put the seed in the ground, either—they'd look at the results of what was planted. The problem is a bad seed was planted in the ground. If the whole garden is bad, we might have to tear it up and start over. That may seem like a discouraging thought, but it's far less discouraging than continually planting the wrong seeds year after year and getting a crop we don't want.

If we want to have happier and more fulfilling lives, we're going to need to deal with this issue head-on. We cannot continue to plant the exact same seeds year after year and expect to get a different harvest—it doesn't work that way. The only way to get a bigger, better harvest is to plant the right kinds of seeds in the right quantities.

GET SOME GOOD SEEDS IN THE GROUND

If we want different circumstances in our lives, we'll need to plant some different seeds. Do you want people to love you more? Well, you now know what kind of seed to plant. You want a promotion at work? Try helping someone else get promoted. Is your spouse not treating you the way you want to be treated? It's time to dig out the hoe and plant a fifty-pound bag of genetically modified "spouse seed." The applications of this principle are endless. If you think about it, this is a very empowering principle because it puts us in the driver's seat of our lives (my favorite place to be). We no longer have to wonder why we're getting the results we are with people. And even better, we now know how to get different results.

I know what some of you are thinking. "Yeah, right. Helping someone else get what he wants isn't going to get me any closer to what I want." False! That is why so many people are stuck in the same place year after year. They absolutely refuse to take advantage of the existing spiritual law of sowing and reaping. Instead of fighting it, get on board with God's system!

When we plant good seeds like I'm describing and reap the rewards from those seeds, we stick out from everyone else. We are no longer part of the herd. People identify us as individuals who put the wants and needs of others before ourselves, and that is *very* appealing to others in leadership positions (people able to bless us with good things). People want to promote and follow individuals who care about others. Do you see what I'm talking about here? Just because we don't fully understand how the law works doesn't mean we can't take advantage of it, either. To be honest, I don't completely understand every nuance of how being born again works but here I am, born again.

Wives, do you feel underappreciated at home? Do you know the best way to encourage others to appreciate you more? Show more appreciation to the members of your family. That's right, start sowing what you want to get in return. If what you're currently doing isn't getting you the appreciation you desire, there is no reason *not* to change how you operate. Trying to force people to appreciate you is exhausting, and the appreciation you *might* get in return isn't sincere anyway—what's the point in spending any more time pursuing it that way? Instead, start getting some "appreciation seed" in the ground and watch it grow over time.

If we want better results with people, we will need to start sowing good seeds into them—things like love, appreciation, and patience (among others). As you read through the remainder of this book, I encourage you to look for ideas you can use to sow into others—and do so liberally. The more good seeds you put in your garden, the bigger harvest you'll have.

BE PATIENT

Just as it takes time between planting a physical garden and harvesting a crop, it takes time between planting and harvesting what we've sown in our lives. In our example of the farmer planting corn seeds, you would think him a little odd if he went out the next day after planting, got on his tractor, and prepared to harvest all of his corn. It doesn't work that way with a physical garden, and it doesn't work that way with a spiritual one, either.

If you remember our Scripture from Galatians 6:9 (TLB), Paul said, "And let us not get tired of doing what is right, for after a while we will reap a harvest of blessing if we don't get discouraged and give up." There is a time between sowing and reaping, and Paul encouraged us not to get discouraged and give up. If he warned us, there must be a possibility that we could give up on our garden before it is ready to harvest. I don't know about you, but I don't want to go through all of the trouble of planting and tending a garden, only to get little or no results because I gave up on it. Talk about a recipe for frustration!

Do not give up on your garden! Your crop might not be ready to harvest next week, or next month, but every day you are closer to your harvest than you have ever been. Remember, we are told (in Hebrews

6:11–12, NKJV), "And we desire that each one of you show the same diligence to the full assurance of hope until the end, that you do not become sluggish, but imitate those who through faith and patience inherit the promises." Be patient. Don't give up on your crop. In due season, you will have your harvest.

8

Selfishness Is at the Root of Most Problems

Do you want to know the chief cause of most of the problems in the world today? It isn't a lack of money. It isn't a shortage of food. It isn't even the political system in your country. The number one cause of problems in the world today is selfishness. Google defines selfish as this:

> *selfish:* *lacking consideration for others; concerned chiefly with one's own personal profit or pleasure*

Some synonyms are as follows: egotistical, self-centered, self-absorbed, self-seeking, self-serving; inconsiderate, thoughtless, uncaring; mean, greedy. Yikes! That sounds exactly like what we are *not* supposed to be like, and it's for a reason.

We are told (in James 3:16, NKJV), "For where envy and self-seeking exist, confusion and every evil thing are there." Read that again. Where selfishness exists, *every* evil thing is there. Think of something evil or wrong. If you were to trace it back to its origin, you would find someone being selfish. Greed? Selfishness. Adultery? Selfishness. Gossip? Selfishness. If we were to dig into anything evil, we would find a person who says "I," "me," and "mine" a whole lot, which is a key indicator that they are being selfish.

Selfishness may manifest itself in many not-so-obvious ways, too.

Did you know that focusing too much on what other people need to do for us (for example, how they treat us) is a form of selfishness? That's right, when we get overly focused on our own needs, we open the door to many of the unsavory side effects that come along with being selfish. If we are chiefly concerned with only our own needs, we're more apt to become offended and angry when the people around us don't provide what we're looking for. Anger and offense will then lead us to much larger problems—and it all started because we put ourselves at the center of our universe, instead of God.

I have found in my own life, the more focused I am on myself, the less happy I become. I think this is because I simply give more place to my own desires, which causes them to become bigger in my own mind. The more I think about what I want, and the less I think about others, the less I'm apt to do things for others—not realizing that sowing into other people's lives is one of the primary ways to experience more fulfillment in my own life. It doesn't help that we are born with a selfish nature, either. That is why we can't base all of our decisions on how we feel—we were born with a broken compass!

Another common form of selfishness is not obeying God because we are too concerned with how we are going to look to those around us. Personally speaking, there have been many times when I've felt led to do something—perhaps share the gospel with someone I don't know—and I've ignored the leading because I was too concerned with how uncomfortable I might feel while doing it. That's pure selfishness. I was more concerned with how I felt than with how God wanted to minister to the other individual through me. If we are unable to act because we are overly concerned with how something makes us look to those around us, we will never be used by God to the degree we want.

As Christians, if we know that every evil thing accompanies selfishness, we should stay as far away from it as possible. Sadly, this is not the case for many people. In general, if God instructs us to stay away from something (either through His Word or His Spirit), it's not to deny us of happiness—it's to keep us safe!

One thing we should get firmly established in our minds is that God is on our side. Would He really have orchestrated this whole redemptive plan with Jesus if He wasn't? He put a plan in place from the very fall of man in order to reconcile us with Him, sent Himself as a human being to die for our rebellion because we could never fix it ourselves, and then we question whether He has our best interests at heart? We are His family! If He instructs us to stay away from something, it's because He's trying to save us from a whole lot of heartache on the back end.

Figure 5 demonstrates how we should live our lives concerning things we are instructed to stay away from. We should identify the temptation, realize God is trying to help us, and then get as far away from the bad behavior as possible. Unfortunately, a lot of people approach these things like in figure 6. They get as close to the bad behavior as they can while still being "technically" safe from it. Can we all agree that

Figure 5

the closer you are to a potential problem, the easier it is to "fall" into it? If you don't want to have premarital sex, then you shouldn't skirt the edge of that cliff. Put safeguards in place to force yourself to stay far away from it. Like I said previously, it's easier to drive past the grocery store than it is to walk past the cookie aisle. Do not put yourself in a position where one little slip up can cause you to completely fall into the ditch—give yourself a buffer that can help protect you. Don't

Figure 6

entertain the thoughts and walk close to the edge of the cliff.

It seems like people are hesitant to want to become more unselfish because they don't think they'll get their needs met. Nothing could be farther from the truth. We are told (in Proverbs 11:25, NKJV), "The generous soul will be made rich, and he who waters will also be watered himself." If we're generous with our resources (time, energy, and money), we will be "watered," too. And not only will our needs be met, but we also will have cultivated many mutually beneficial relationships along the way. It's a win-win situation, so we'd be foolish not to do it.

Would you like God to lift you up (promote you and use you more)? Do you know the type of person He's looking for? Someone with humility (a modest or low view of one's own importance). In James 4:10 (NKJV), we read, "Humble yourselves in the sight of the Lord, and He will lift you up." The Amplified Bible puts it this way, "Humble yourselves [with an attitude of repentance and insignificance] in the presence of the Lord, and He will exalt you [He will lift you up, He will give you purpose]." Humility is a prerequisite for being exalted and lifted up by God—because why would He want to promote someone into an area of more influence if He knew that person would primarily be concerned only with himself? Sounds like the definition of a bad leader to me. If we're frustrated by our seeming lack of progress in any area of our lives, we may want to check our "selfishness meter"—it might be running a little hot. We need to double-check how much emphasis we are putting on our own wants and desires.

In Philippians 2:3–4 (NKJV), it is written: "Let nothing be done through selfish ambition or conceit, but in lowliness of mind let each esteem others better than himself. Let each of you look out not only for his own interests, but also for the interests of others." When we are selfish, we are more likely to look down on others. We quickly forget that every good thing we have and know is a gift from the Lord. Paul instructed us to walk in humility—get the focus off of just ourselves and onto how living blessed also enables us to be more of a blessing to the people around us. God's uses for a person like this are nearly limitless because He doesn't have to be concerned about the person's selfishness getting in the way and messing everything up.

As I said earlier, we're born selfish—and some people never grow out of it. It takes practice to learn to be less selfish. It seems to be easier for some people than others; but innately, we are chiefly concerned with our own wants and needs, and it takes some work to reprogram our minds. In my opinion, the most effective way to change the selfish pattern is to realize all of the opportunities that are available to you by becoming unselfish (chapter 1). Renew your mind to what God says about selfishness and use biblical examples to help guide you as you attempt to walk humbly with God in your daily life. Apply the principles you'll learn in this book and make a habit out of them.

If we only interact with people when we need something from them, is there any wonder why we run into problems? We are being selfish and reaping the rewards of what selfishness brings—resistance, strife, unhappiness, and selfishness from the people around us. We are planting a bad seed in the ground and harvesting the wrong kind of crop. What's the answer? Sow unselfishness and you'll reap unselfishness in return. In a later chapter, I'll talk in more detail about how to be less selfish and give you specific examples of what you can do to break down some of the barriers selfishness creates in our lives.

To become more successful at dealing with people, we will need to start thinking more about what others need or want, and less about ourselves. If we are unwilling to do this, we never will connect with people on a deep enough level to truly influence them to the degree that we want to.

9

Learn to Love People

In order to be successful with people over the long haul, we're going to have to learn how to love them. We don't have to love all of the things they do, but we do need to love them for who they are: one-of-a-kind beings created by God for a purpose. Each and every person is an absolute masterpiece. We are the apex of the known universe! We are told (in Luke 12:7, NKJV) that "the very hairs of your head are all numbered." God loves people so much that He even knows how many hairs are on their heads! God is all about loving people—He's the ultimate people person.

Believe it or not, this was the last chapter I wrote for the book. After I finished the first couple of drafts, I felt like something was still missing—something so core to being better with people that to omit it would be a serious misstep on my part. After much prayer, it hit me—I hadn't talked about love, yet! I'm not talking about a weird kind of love here, either. I'm talking about the God kind of love in which you *choose* to genuinely care about the wellbeing of others and unselfishly put their needs above your own, even when their actions don't deserve it.

Any book written with the intent of helping you to become better with people that omits the topic of love is missing a core principle that will help you to achieve long-term results with others year after year. Trying to become more skillful with people without addressing the love issue is like putting a Band-Aid on a broken arm—you need to get at the root of the problem if you truly want to fix it.

We need to become "all in" when it comes to loving people. We know that if we want to lose weight and keep it off, we have to permanently change how we eat and exercise. Similarly, we need to permanently change our view of people if we want to reap the long-term benefits (for them and us) of the change. We absolutely can decide that people are important (after all, Jesus died for them) and that we want to do everything in our power to help them, to influence them, and to sow into their lives. We can decide to love them—just as Jesus did.

If you're a parent, you know exactly the type of love I'm talking about here. Kids don't always say and do things that make you happy. Do you stop loving them? No. You've decided you're in it for the long haul, and you still love them through whatever situation you're currently experiencing. You may not like what they are doing at the moment, but you still have an unshakable love for them deep down inside of you that keeps you invested in the relationship and there for them when things turn around. You have decided to love them, even when they sometimes don't deserve it.

For many of us, the problem is we've never truly learned to love others. We don't hate people, but we've entered into this sort of uneasy truce with them where we'll tolerate them as long as everything is going well. When things get tough, though, we lack the heart to get us through whatever adverse situation we're currently facing. We've already decided up front that we don't really care for people that much, so why should we work hard at cultivating or fixing our relationships with them?

Some of you may be wondering about now, how in the heck are you supposed to walk this out in real life? Good question! Fortunately for us, God didn't leave us hanging here. If you look in Romans 5:5 (NKJV), you'll read, "Now hope does not disappoint, because the love of God has been poured out in our hearts by the Holy Spirit who was given to us." God has given us *His* love! If you are born again, you already have the love of God inside you. You may not feel any different, but you have available to you *God's* ability to love people, even when you don't think you can. Whew, crisis averted—we don't have to do this on our own!

Without an awareness of God's love in your heart, you eventually will reach an end to what you're capable of doing in your own power. Eventually, you're going to become tired, lonely, and angry—what then? If God's love hasn't been cultivated and given priority, whatever is dominating your heart is going to come out because you don't have the energy to force yourself to do the right thing anymore. There is a better way that we've already talked about: Get a heart transplant! We need to learn to love people. Then, getting along with them will just be a simple outgrowth of who we are as people—it's at our very core.

As Christians, we are supposed to be Christlike. One of the major pillars of Jesus's ministry while He was here on the earth was compassion. Wherever Jesus went, He healed the sick and taught people the truth, so they could be set free from the junk of this world. When we confessed Jesus as our Lord, we literally were saying: "You are in charge now. What You say, I'll do." Read through the first four books of the New Testament (Matthew, Mark, Luke, and John) to find out exactly how Jesus related to people—He loved them!

THE NEW COMMANDMENT

We've been instructed by Jesus Himself to love others. Jesus said (in John 13:34–35, NKJV): "A new commandment I give to you, that you love one another; as I have loved you, that you also love one another. By this all will know that you are My disciples, if you have love for one another." Jesus was talking to His disciples here, but He didn't limit our love to *only* fellow Christians. We know this because in Matthew 22:39 (NKJV), Jesus said the second great commandment is "You shall love your neighbor as yourself." From God's standpoint, loving each other is not optional—it's essential to the Christian's life. Love is what's going to keep us going when things aren't going our way and when people are being difficult.

Without making the decision to love people, we'll be tempted to cut and run when situations get tough. People are going to say and do things that are hurtful—love them anyway. Without the premeditated decision to love others, we're going to quickly run out of our own "steam" and start making decisions based on what's best for ourselves, not what's best for others.

Scriptures like John 13:34 have lost their "bite" for many people because it's very easy to read them and think to yourself, "Yeah, I know that—I'm supposed to love other people." Well, do you love other people? I've found in my short forty years on the earth that definitions of "love" vary greatly depending on someone's upbringing and personal experiences in life. Let's take a look at God's definition of love and see how we measure up to it.

GOD'S DEFINITION OF LOVE

We need to get settled on the "official" definition of love before we decide we are going to operate in it. I warn you, however, that God's definition is not for the faint of heart. God's kind of love is not based on a feeling, and it's not based on what others do for you first.

In 1 Corinthians 13:4–7 (TLB), we are given God's definition of love: "Love is very patient and kind, never jealous or envious, never boastful or proud, never haughty or selfish or rude. Love does not demand its own way. It is not irritable or touchy. It does not hold grudges and will hardly even notice when others do it wrong. It is never glad about injustice, but rejoices whenever truth wins out. If you love someone, you will be loyal to him no matter what the cost. You will always believe in him, always expect the best of him, and always stand your ground in defending him." Now, based on that definition of love, would you say that you love the people around you? Personally speaking, I continually fall short with some people—but at least I know what I'm shooting for now!

There are so many life-changing concepts in that Scripture that we could probably write an entire book (maybe someone has) picking each one of them apart. Are you jealous or envious of someone? If so, you're not operating in love. Do you constantly demand your own way? Well, according to God's definition, you're not operating in love. This Scripture can be used as the measuring stick for us to determine if we are truly loving people the way God wants us to love them.

God's kind of love is completely selfless. If your family operated in this kind of love, can you imagine how pleasant it would be in your home each and every day? If people in general operated like this, it would truly be heaven on earth—but that's the way it's supposed to be right now! Instead, what we have are a bunch of selfish, impatient, jealous individuals interacting with each other, and we wonder why we have so many problems!

LOVE IS A CHOICE

There are two types of love: the emotional type and the decision type. The emotional type of love is a fleeting feeling. It's typically controlled by circumstances and how someone else makes you feel. We've all been there: the beginnings of a blossoming relationship or a crush on someone we find attractive. During these times, we are filled with emotion because things are new and exciting. The problem is those times eventually end. What then? If we only love someone because of circumstances or how they make us feel, we are going to have a rude awakening when those feelings are no longer there. What happens after the "honeymoon phase" of a marriage is over and it's time to get down to business—working a job, raising kids, and deciding what to eat for dinner?

The last thing I want to sound like is that I'm advocating we all model ourselves after Mr. Spock of the '60s television show *Star Trek*. In this show, Mr. Spock was half Vulcan, a race of beings devoted to the eradication of emotions. God didn't create us to be emotionless! Emotions can be normal and healthy. They also are fleeting and unreliable. Jesus felt emotions, but He was never led by His emotions. As Christians, we are instructed to be led by the Spirit of God—nothing else.

God's definition of love is what I'm calling decision-based love. When you decide to love someone, it is not dependent on the other person—it's 100 percent you. You can intellectually choose to love others regardless of how they treat you. I know in practice that can sound unrealistic but that's exactly the kind of love God showed us by sending Jesus to die for us. He had no reason to do it. We already had separated ourselves from Him through sin. We see many examples in the Old Testament of humans wholesale turning their backs on Him and going their own way. He had every reason to write us off, but He didn't. He didn't because He loved us with the type of love I'm describing. When He created man, He decided He was going to love us. He loved us so much that He put a plan in place to reconcile us to Himself through Jesus, and this plan took a *really* long time to come to pass. He never gave up. He patiently waited for the plan to unfold because His love for us wasn't based on our actions—it was based on His decision.

I know what some of you are thinking. "Well, you don't know the type of person I live with." No, I don't. But I do know what God says about your situation, and He says to love the other person anyway. If *both* people aren't loving each other, I can guarantee you the relationship isn't going to work out. If you do your part, you might be surprised to find out how effective it can be at influencing the other person to change. If you only love someone back when they love you, you'll find yourself being completely dissatisfied over and over again. This is why people bounce around from relationship to relationship. People want the "fix" of emotional love and bail when that fizzles out. This is a recipe for a lonely, dissatisfied life.

Make the choice to love people—not because they deserve it, but because God instructed us to do so and it's the right thing to do. When times get tough, this decision will allow you to stick with them when everyone else around them falls away. Decision-based love is what separates Christians from the rest of the world—*we love people*. People are our business because people are God's business. The only way to reach people to the extent that God wants us to is to choose to love them, warts and all.

LET GOD CHANGE YOU FROM THE INSIDE

Now that we know how important loving people is, let's talk about making the internal adjustments necessary to decide to love people more. The good news here is that it's pretty easy to become better at loving people. Actually, if you do what I'm about to tell you, the change will be almost effortless on your part—no white-knuckling it through life trying to love people like you're supposed to.

The first way to change our hearts toward people is to spend time in God's Word. God's Word shows us who we really are, not who people say we are. It helps to strip away all of that junk that has built up in our hearts, so we can become tender toward people again. It teaches us how to forgive. It teaches us that any circumstances here on the earth are temporary. It teaches us to invest in people because they are the only form of "eternal currency" there is—everything else is going to end up rubble.

Jesus said (in John 8:32, NKJV), "And you shall know the truth, and the truth shall make you free." If we want to be set free from our worldly thinking toward people, we need to get the truth inside of us. God's Word is one of the primary mechanisms for getting truth in us, but we need to read or listen to it.

A second way to help change our hearts toward people is to sit under anointed teaching at a local church. God has given people special gifts in order to help train us—make sure to take advantage of that. If we wanted to learn how to be better at playing the piano, we'd go find a teacher. Same thing goes for being a Christian. If we want to be better Christians and to be better with people, we need to go find someone who's farther down the road to help us.

Not all pastors are the same. It's been my experience that certain teachers resonate with me more than others. First and foremost, we always want to be led. Ask God if you're in the right place for you. Or, if you're not attending a church at all, ask God to lead you to the right one. He knows where you should be, and it'd be foolish to waste years going to a church that you weren't even supposed to be at in the first place.

Another way to help change our hearts is to supplement all of the great teaching we are hearing at our local churches with teachers from different places around the country. With the technology we have today, we can access years of archived teachings from individuals who have a proven track record of changing people's lives for the better. Ask around your Christian circles, and people will happily share their favorite teachers with you. Doing this allows us to take advantage of the gifts God has given people who don't even live close to us—how awesome is that?

As we pour in the Word, we'll watch it push out all of the other junk—no more forcing ourselves to do the right thing. Instead, we'll find that we *want* to do the right thing because God has been slowly changing us from the inside out. Little by little, we'll start noticing that we have more patience and tolerance for people. What's happening? God is changing our hearts, and all we had to do was grow in knowledge and understanding of Him. Just as our hearts had grown cold, they also can be warmed up again!

10

The Golden Rule

Part of me almost feels embarrassed for including this chapter in the book. "Do unto others as you'd have them do unto you" is something we've heard since we were kids, but because so few people incorporate this principle into their daily lives, I feel I have to put it in here. Remember, just because you've heard something before doesn't mean you know it. Don't get trapped in the I've-heard-that-before way of thinking—that's dangerous. Don't tell someone you know this concept, *show* the person that you know it through your actions.

In general, people aren't failing in their relationships with others because they need some new, completely radical approach to the problem. It's actually quite the opposite. Most people just need to be reminded of the basics and then encouraged to do them. The Golden Rule is one of those foundational principles in life, but how many people actually apply it on a regular basis? I know I don't do it to the degree I should.

Jesus said (in Luke 6:31, NKJV), "And just as you want men to do to you, you also do to them." This is Jesus, God in the flesh, telling us how we should treat other people. It's easy to quickly read this Scripture and agree with it, but it's a whole other thing to model our lives after it.

If everyone operated in accordance with the Golden Rule, can you imagine how amazing life would be? People wouldn't spread lies about you, because they wouldn't want someone to spread lies about them.

People would attend service at their home church more often because if they were the pastor, they'd want people to show up, too. Giving to others (money, time, etc.) would be a piece of cake because we like it when people give to us. If we were to really think about it, doing the right thing with people starts with applying the Golden Rule in every interaction we have.

Think of one stressed relationship in your life right now. I can almost guarantee you that one or both of you are directly violating the Golden Rule. I know what some of you are thinking. "But you don't know what I have to put up with!" I don't. But I'd challenge you by asking: How's your current strategy with that person working out, so far? You've identified that this relationship is a source of stress in your life. Dealing with it in a healthy way will increase your quality of life. You do this with enough relationships and, all of a sudden, you're much happier than you've ever been.

We shouldn't be too quick to point the finger at the other fellow as the source of all of our problems. It's been my experience that we have a part to play in the state of every relationship in our lives. Ask yourself, "What have I done to contribute to the current state of this relationship?" Have you been applying the Golden Rule with this person or have you been selfish? If you've been selfish, there's a cure for that. If you need some tools to help you fix the damaged relationship, this book can help—keep reading.

When you go to work tomorrow, start analyzing your interactions with your co-workers. Are you treating them like you want to be treated? I know this may sound sort of silly, but this is how we change things in our lives—we identify a problem, come up with a plan to fix it, and then implement the plan. Are you short with people? Do you talk down to them? If so, it's causing you problems. Ask yourself, "How would I want them to treat me?" and then start treating them that way. It'll change your life.

11

The Power of Words

I'm going to tell you up front: This is one of the most important chapters in the book (and I think they are all important). There is a lot to digest, but if you internalize what I'm saying, it will change your life—more so than probably anything we have talked about up to this point. If we are doing everything else right but not strictly controlling the words that are coming out of our mouths, we will not achieve the level of success (with anything) that we're looking for in life. That's not even the worst of it! If we aren't actively managing what we say, we are unintentionally causing problems for ourselves—problems that could be avoided just by controlling our mouths.

There are only two ways to get things done in life: what we say and what we do. There's no other way. If we are trying to do our best at controlling our actions but not putting the same effort into controlling our mouths, it's akin to fortifying a castle with one-hundred-foot walls but leaving the front gate wide open! We are giving the enemy (Satan or the devil) direct access to our lives by not putting any safeguards between our brains and our mouths.

As tough as this may be to hear, we are probably the cause of most of the problems in our lives. Our inability to control our own words (and actions) is causing us great harm—and it's no one's fault but our own. I know there are some exceptions, but personally speaking, I can look back and trace most of my failures to my own actions—usually my words. I'm convinced that for some individuals, the quality of their lives would immediately increase if they just stopped talking.

It's written in Proverbs 12:14 (NKJV), "A man will be satisfied with good by the fruit of his mouth, and the recompense of a man's hands will be rendered to him." What kind of "fruit" (results of your words) are you getting in your life? If it's not what you want, look no further than your mouth.

Think about it for yourself. How many people do you have issues with because of what they have said to you? If you're like many people, you probably have a decent-size list. We avoid people because they hurt our feelings, we cut people out of our lives because of things they've said, and we damage relationships with people who used to be close to us because of words that are spoken.

Let's be mature enough to realize that it isn't always the other guy's fault, either. Communication typically breaks down because of *both* parties, not just one. We have a part to play in the state of our relationships. If we aren't controlling our own mouths, we are, at the very least, pouring gasoline on an existing fire—boom!

DEATH AND LIFE

Death and life are in the power of the tongue, and those who love it will eat its fruit.
—*Proverbs 18:21 (NKJV)*

Do you understand the implications of this Scripture? It's literally saying that our mouths have the power to bring more "life" (good things) into our lives or more "death" (bad things) into our lives. We all know this principle to be true because we see it in operation all around us—the smooth talker getting the girl or the job applicant landing the position because he performed so well at the interview. It's everywhere.

To prove this spiritual law, I'd like to challenge you to something. Are you up for it? The next time you go to work, see if you can get fired in less than sixty seconds using only words. Do you think you could do it? I *know* you could. Using nothing more than your mouth, you could lose the main source of income in your life. How can that happen? It's because, as we read in Proverbs, words carry life-and-death power. In my challenge, you could use them to bring a whole lot of death into your life. Sure, every day you may not be saying things that will get you fired, but where are you on the life-death continuum—are the words you say producing more life, or are they producing more death?

Your mouth literally could be killing you: killing your health, killing your finances, killing your relationships, and killing your hope. If you're not happy with the way things are going in your life, I'd first start by looking at what words are coming out of your mouth. Do you have a stressful marriage? What are you saying to each other? Are you upset because you don't have many close friends? How do you talk to people when you're around them? Are you constantly tearing down your children with your words? What kinds of results are you getting from doing that? Do you keep wondering why you don't get the promotion at work? How do you talk to your co-workers? The list goes on and on. If you have never sat down and consciously thought about what you say all day long, you have a great opportunity before you—maybe one of the biggest of your life—because you've been ignoring one of the most powerful tools you have for bringing good things into your life.

We've been focusing on the death part of our words, but Proverbs 18:21 listed both death and life. If you desire to have more life in your life, your mouth is one of the primary vehicles to do that. Just like we can cause ourselves immeasurable harm by not controlling the words we say, we also can proactively bring large amounts of life into our lives by consciously choosing our words thoughtfully and purposefully. While it is critical to avoid speaking in a way that negatively affects our lives, it's just as important to put our mouths to work in a positive direction. Use your mouth to the advantage of yourself and the people around you.

Remember that Jesus said whatever we say and believe, we get (Mark 11:23). If we continually speak life-producing words and believe them, that's what we're going to get. If we continually speak death-filled words and believe them, that's also what we're going to get. It sounds a lot like the spiritual law of sowing and reaping, doesn't it? Over and over, we see in the Bible that there's an emphasis on what we say.

The book of Proverbs is a great source of godly wisdom that has more than twenty Scriptures related to wisely choosing our words. (And that's just out of one book in the Bible!) One example is Proverbs 13:3 (NKJV) where it's written that "He who guards his mouth preserves his life, but he who opens wide his lips shall have destruction." Proverbs 21:23 (NKJV) reads, "Whoever guards his mouth and tongue keeps his soul from troubles." Do you see a pattern here?

People have been killed for what they have said. I'm not sure there is a more clear demonstration of the power of our words than that. When a man is arrested, and before he is asked questions, a police officer must read the Miranda Warning: "You have the right to remain silent. Anything you *say* can and will be used against you in a court of law." If the government can use our own words to convict us of a crime, don't you think regular people in our lives are doing the same thing? We are constantly being judged and convicted by the words that come out of our mouths.

How do great leaders inspire action? They inspire action through their words. They speak, people listen, and then people act on those words. Words are the primary vehicle for getting most anything done in the world. Heck, God *spoke* the world into existence (Genesis 1:3). Never underestimate the power of your words. Speaking the right things can influence the right behavior in other individuals. Revolutions are started with words, and those words usually originate from a single person. Get enough people saying the right things, and you have a revolution on your hands. We literally can change the course of human history with our mouths. Jesus did. Paul the apostle did. Abraham Lincoln did. We have this same power inside of us—our words!

What am I trying to say here? I'm trying to say that if we ignore the power of our words, we are going to pay for it dearly. The price may be lost friends, a broken marriage, unrealized opportunities at work, or even an early grave. Instead, why don't we intelligently manage one of the most powerful weapons we have and use it to guide us into peace, health, and prosperity? The choice and power to do so is firmly in our control.

OUR MOUTHS ARE WEAPONS

One of the worst things you can do for yourself is to let your mouth roam free saying whatever it wants, whenever it wants to say it. Our mouths can cause so many problems that it would be foolish to operate this way. This would be like walking around with a loaded assault rifle everywhere we go, pointing and waving it at people. We would never do that! Why? Because we respect the weapon and the damage it can cause. Our words should be treated with the same respect because they could possess just as much killing power.

Instead, use the power of your mouth as a weapon against adverse situations in your life. I use my mouth to enforce the promises of God—asking for things in prayer and then thanking God as I confess with my mouth that I have them (as Jesus taught). I use my mouth to build myself up using Scripture. I try to the best of my ability to avoid using my mouth against other people, as I've learned through experience that it can cause irreparable damage to myself and others. My ship hasn't arrived but at least it has left the dock—I'm still learning to get better in this area!

Once we choose our words and say them, there is no taking them back. Sure, we can apologize, but the damage is still done. Some words are so painful that the wounds will *never* fully heal, at least not without God's help. Personally speaking, if you say mean and hateful things to me, I'm going to forgive you—but I'm going to choose not to be around you. Why would I? So you can continue to pour more death into me? For people who *have to* be around us (our spouses and our children), the undisciplined use of our mouths can be nearly unbearable and cause long-term, deep-rooted resentment toward us. Be careful! Once the arrow is let go (our words), there's no getting it back.

WORDS ARE SEEDS

Every word that comes out of our mouths is like a seed. We plant bad seeds, we get a bad crop. We plant good seeds, we get a good crop. It's the law of sowing and reaping that I talked about in chapter 7.

Throughout the day, every single interaction we have with people is an opportunity to plant a thistle bush or a beautiful flower—it's our choice. The people around us are our soil, and as we've been learning, we *will* reap what we sow into them. If we plant mercy, we'll get mercy (Matthew 5:7). If we plant hate, we'll get hate. If we plant appreciation, we'll get appreciation. When people plant physical gardens, they choose the exact kinds of plants they want to grow. We can do the same thing in the people around us by choosing what we plant into them.

Put the odds in your favor and proactively seed the ground with the type of crop you want. If you've just started a new job, this is the perfect time to put this principle into practice. Don't hide in your office or cube—get out and plant some seeds! Visit the break room, ask people their names in the elevator, or invite someone you don't know out to lunch. This is what planting seeds looks like in real life. Don't leave your interactions up to chance. Decide when and what type of seed you want to plant and then go do it—you are in control of what you plant and what you harvest. How empowering!

OUR MOUTHS ARE THE STEERING WHEELS OF OUR LIVES

Control your mouth, control your life. The apostle James said (in James 3:3–5, TLB): "We can make a large horse turn around and go wherever we want by means of a small bit in his mouth. And a tiny rudder makes a huge ship turn wherever the pilot wants it to go, even though the winds are strong. So also the tongue is a small thing, but what enormous damage it can do. A great forest can be set on fire by one tiny spark."

Your mouth, like the small rudder of a ship, is guiding the course of your life. If you aren't exerting control over it, your mouth is likely taking you to places you don't want to go in the same way that a ship with no one steering it would. We *cannot* ignore the words we say—that would be like ignoring the steering wheel of the car while we're driving down the road. Wouldn't you think someone was crazy if he said he doesn't use the steering wheel of his car when he drives? Well, that's about how crazy we'd be not to use the steering wheels of our lives (our mouths) while we are "driving" through life. Is there any wonder why people have so many "accidents" while living their lives? Use your steering wheel, man! It's not only safer for you, but it's safer for everyone else on the road with you. I don't want you to run into me because you don't know how to use the primary mechanism for guiding your life. We are all on the road of life together; our inability to steer doesn't only affect us, it affects everyone else around us. Be a good driver and use your mouth wisely!

OUR FAITH COMES BY WORDS WE HEAR

We learn in Romans 10:17 (NKJV) that "faith comes by hearing, and hearing by the word of God." In order to become settled in godly faith—faith that produces God's results in our lives—we need to hear (or read) the Word of God. How would you even know what God has promised you if you've never heard anyone tell you about it? This is why reading our Bibles and attending church regularly is so important. If we have little Word coming in, we have little faith in it.

Did you know you can actually hear yourself speaking things that are contrary to the Word of God and develop faith in them? If we spend all day talking about how sick we are, how broke we are, how we never get any breaks, and how we have rotten kids, we are making the wrong confession. Our faith now comes by hearing the wrong words as we are using our own mouths against us.

A pastor I was listening to one time used this definition of faith (from Hebrews 10:23, KJV): a confident expectation. I like that. When we pray and are in faith, we are confidently expecting or believing we have what we asked for. By doing a little digging on blueletterbible.org, we can see this same Greek word "elpis" most commonly is translated as "hope." This word also is used in the Bible as "expectation of evil, fear" or "expectation of good, hope." We can confess words of godly faith and expect to see good things in our lives, or we can convince ourselves that we are going to fail. We confidently expect our condition to stay the same, and it *does* come to pass. Our job as Christians is to understand this principle, find out what God says about us, and then start saying that about ourselves.

As I finish this chapter, I want to make one more significant point, and that is this: Your mouth can prevent you from walking in God's blessings—it can counteract them. I know that may sound new to some people, but hear me out on this. You could have all of the opportunities in the world divinely arranged for you, and you could undermine each one of them with your words. You could have God supernaturally arrange a meeting with your future spouse, and you could be so offensive with your words that the person is not interested in you romantically. If you believe God heals, you could receive physical healing and then speak nothing but unbelief with your mouth and counteract your faith. The bottom line is that words are extremely important, not just from a physical standpoint but from a spiritual standpoint, as well. Take heed to *every* word that comes out of your mouth, because life and death literally depend on it.

12

We Have a 'Bank Account' with Every Person We Meet

I like it when intangible realities can be represented with something tangible that I'm familiar with. As an example, remember (back in chapter 7) how we compared the law of sowing and reaping to a physical garden in a backyard? Comparisons like this are useful because they help me to understand something that may be a bit confusing by using something I already understand. Another analogy that can be helpful to use when talking about our interactions with people is a bank account.

Most everybody, I hope, understands how a bank account works. You open an account with a financial institution, and then you can start making deposits into or withdrawals from your account. If you try to withdraw too much, at best you can't get it, and at worst you get charged an overdraft fee. And just as our bank accounts work from a financial standpoint, our "bank accounts" with people work in a similar way.

With every interaction, we either make a deposit into or a withdrawal from the individual we're interacting with. Every time we ask someone for something, we make a withdrawal—sometimes small, sometimes huge. Every time we tear down or criticize someone, we make a withdrawal. Eventually, if we haven't made enough deposits into a person's account, we get into the red (overdraft), and that's when we start experiencing problems.

When you see certain people coming toward you, do you ever think to yourself, "Oh great, what do they want now?" Every time they come around, they always want something from you, and they never seem to be around to help you with anything you want. What's the problem? The problem is they only make withdrawals from your account instead of putting some deposits in there, too. The result is the relationship is strained, and neither of you is getting the best out of each other.

Do you have a strained relationship in your life? Does it seem like the people around you aren't giving you their best? Do people you know try to avoid you? Or, do you have problems trying to lead groups of volunteers or co-workers on the job? Your bank account with these individuals might be completely empty.

OK, so how can you fix it? Intentionally make deposits to build up your reserves with the people around you. If you put it off until you need a large withdrawal, it's too late. We'll go into much more detail about exactly how to make deposits into an account, but for right now, some simple examples of deposits could be making people feel important, acknowledging specific things they've done recently, or even finding out what their favorite candy is and getting them a bag of it. It doesn't have to be huge. People are so starved for positive human affirmation that nearly anything is a giant leap in the right direction.

What I like about the bank account analogy is that it gains momentum over time if you have a group of individuals who operate like this. Deposits come more often and in larger sums to the point where people are working harder than ever because they are happier than they have ever been. Everyone's account is nearly overflowing. In return, people are willing to do whatever is required—because the withdrawals don't even bring them close to zero. See how awesome this is?

In corporate America, I often hear about "making this place the best place to work." How do you actually make a company or church the best place to work? It doesn't come by making a slick mission statement, though those are important. It doesn't come by mandating "This shall be the best place to work!" The *only* way to make some place the best place to work is by changing people's hearts and teaching the importance of what we are covering in this book. Then *they* take the information they've learned and *make* your company the best place to work. It is not management's responsibility to make your organization the best place to work—it's everyone's responsibility. Management does have a part to play, for sure, but it's no more important than each employee's part. Having a group of individuals who are aware of their bank accounts with each other and consciously focused on keeping those accounts healthy will have a greater impact on making a company a great place to work than trying to dictate it from the top. Remember, action is what produces results (not just talking or thinking about everything we should do but don't).

When I worked for Hewlett-Packard as a software developer, I ran into a situation where I had to consciously make some deposits into an individual's account to patch up a rough first impression he had of me. We got off to a bad start, and I knew that without intervention it was going to stay bad or potentially get worse.

"Alex" was a good employee—a bit rough around the edges but a good guy in most respects. He was a hard worker and genuinely wanted to do the right thing for the company. When I was first introduced to him, I was a little overpowering when we initially discussed the direction I thought the team should go. As the technical leader, part of my responsibilities was to help set the course of the team; and looking back, I was a little too "energetic" (that's code for "said stuff I shouldn't have"). I could tell immediately after the conversation that he didn't particularly like what I had to say, because his demeanor changed. From then on, he never talked much when I was around, and his entire countenance and the way he carried himself was much more reserved—I had hurt him a little.

I had a choice to make: I could forget about it and hope my relationship with Alex got better on its own, or I could proactively try to patch things up using the limited skills I had at the time. I knew from experience that most people aren't real good about forgiving and moving on, so it was probably going to fall on me to fix the problem (which is probably the right thing, since it was my mouth that caused the issue in the first place). I immediately got to work thinking about how I could build up my bank account with him.

Looking back, patching up the relationship was much easier than I thought it would be. I'd stop by Alex's cube every other day or so and tell him how great of a job he was doing or ask him questions about his personal life to get to know him a little better. I made an effort to deposit into his account—and it worked! After maybe a month, he probably even considered me a friend. Because of those simple deposits, he started smiling every time he saw me, and he'd even stop by my cube occasionally just to strike up a conversation.

A lot of the stressful relationships in our lives could be improved with a simple game plan for how to go about making the correct types and amounts of deposits into the other person's account. I recognize that every relationship won't be as easy to fix, but I've never seen a relationship hurt by trying to build someone up.

Don't be like the people who expect others to "just get over" problems between you and them. Mark my words: Unresolved issues cause resentment and grow into bigger problems over time. The best time to deal with them is when they are little, tiny problems—when you can come right in and pluck them out of the ground. If you wait too long and let offense and resentment build, you'll have to bring in a crane to pull them out. It's so much easier if we identify a problem with a person early on and then proactively work to fix it. After one week, a resolution may take the form of a sincere apology. After ten years, we may need help from a professional and a ton of dynamite to get that sucker out of the ground. Oh, how I wish I were kidding.

As I wrap up this chapter, I'd like to encourage you to actively manage the bank accounts in your life. You have one of these accounts with every single person you meet. The people close to you matter the most, and those account balances should be checked on a daily basis. Accounts with co-workers and acquaintances can go a little longer. As a husband, I know that if I let my balance get a little too low with my wife, she'll let me know. If it gets really low, I need to start making larger deposits. It's much easier to make small deposits regularly than to try to make huge ones at larger intervals. After all, you can only buy so many ponies for someone.

If you're a parent, realize the principles we're talking about here apply to our children, too. Just because our children are young doesn't mean we can violate every rule of interpersonal communication with them. They are adults in training. It is our responsibility to equip them for the real world. The best way to equip them for dealing with people when they leave home is by demonstrating the proper behavior with them while they are living with us. We don't want them to have to learn it the hard way, by themselves, when great opportunities are passing them by because they don't understand the fundamentals of dealing with others. Teach them about bank accounts and how to deposit into the accounts of their friends and teachers. If I had the skills I possess now when I was younger, my life would look different (in a good way) than it does today—and I have a pretty good life. Do your kids a favor and teach them this material.

Part 2: Concrete Application

13

The Three 'Do Nots'

All right, we are to the part of the book where hopefully we've all been convinced that having better people skills is important and that we can greatly increase the quality of our lives and the lives of everyone around us if we change how we interact with each other. If you haven't been convinced, keep reading because I'll continually try to demonstrate why having more skill with people will make you happier, healthier, and more financially prosperous.

I know some like to say there are no absolutes in life, but I disagree. We know from chapter 6 that people are predictable, and human nature hasn't changed very much, if at all, in thousands of years. We know that people don't like certain behaviors; so if we want to stay in good graces with them, we should avoid those behaviors. I'm calling a group of these behaviors the three "do nots."

DO NOT CRITICIZE PEOPLE

Most people are familiar with Nike's slogan "Just do it!" Well, my slogan for this section is "Criticism—just *don't* do it!" Let's start by defining what it means to criticize. Google defines criticize this way:

> *criticize:* indicate the faults of (someone or something) in a disapproving way

Some synonyms of criticize are as follows: condemn, attack, lambaste, rail against, pour scorn on, disparage, denigrate, give bad press to, and run down. These all sound really, really bad, and I hope we all can agree that we should *not* operate this way as men and women of God.

Let there be no mistake about what we are talking about here. Criticism's sole purpose is to run down or wound another person. It's mean-spirited and typically is used as an outlet for anger and frustration. It damages relationships and creates barriers in organizations. As Christians, we do not criticize people to their faces *or* behind their backs. No more "roast pastor" for lunch after your Sunday service!

As leaders and managers, we sometimes need to correct people we are influencing. Correction is normal, is one of our primary responsibilities as leaders, and can be done in such a way that our intent is conveyed *and* the recipient of the correction saves face. Criticism, as a form of correction, is the opposite. Its goal is to inflict enough damage to another person that he or she will obey out of fear. It's used liberally in top-down organizations like the military and can be effective at getting a quick fix to a problem. After all, who likes to be run down in front of other people? There are much more effective forms of correction available to us, however: inspiration, encouragement, and mentorship (just to name a few). These forms have less negative, long-term repercussions than criticism.

The problem with criticism is that if you choose to criticize, you lose the goodwill of the person you're criticizing. Instead of having an ally, you now have a potential enemy. Criticize someone enough and you're likely to find yourself in a situation where a person not only *wants* to see you fail but will do everything in his or her power to see it come to pass. It creates an adversarial environment at the workplace and is counterproductive. Think about the Opportunity Tree we talked about at the beginning of the book. Continually criticizing a person damages that branch of your tree. Do you think I'm going to recommend you for a job opportunity if all you've done is criticize me for the last ten years? No way! People don't realize how many opportunities pass them by because of things like this.

I have worked with many software developers over the past fourteen years who have made it their personal duty to criticize the work of everyone else around them. They typically are smart and gifted at what they do and use that as their license to tear down everyone else. I suspect this phenomenon is not specific to developing software, either. As a result, the very people whom everyone else should be seeking out for help and support are actively avoided as much as possible because no one wants to deal with them. Sound familiar? They have created barriers in the organization, and as a result, the team isn't as effective as it could be.

Criticism is counterproductive and wastes a lot of time and emotional energy, too. Criticism causes people to want to defend themselves—it derails any progress that was being made before the criticism occurred. We've probably all seen this play out: The team is gathered together for a weekly staff meeting. People begin explaining what they've been working on, when someone decides he is going to criticize an individual. At this point, the person being criticized enters survival mode and is more concerned with saving face than having a productive meeting. I've seen entire meetings wasted on a couple of people going back and forth trying to defend themselves and the decisions they made. All of it could have been avoided if the person would have chosen not to criticize. Choosing not to criticize is easy to do and is effective at keeping the goodwill of people around you.

Many people take criticisms personally regardless of our intentions—it's like picking a fight with them. Even if we try to play the "constructive-criticism" card (try to "help" them by giving them negative feedback), people don't like it. As a general rule, people *never* like to be told they are wrong and *never* like to be criticized for anything they do. Humans, in general, just don't like it. It doesn't mean we can never correct someone; it just means we have to be careful how we do it.

If we choose to ignore human nature, we are setting the odds against us. Why not use our newfound understanding of people to our advantage? Get the results we want *and* build stronger teams while we're at it. It isn't an "or" type of decision we have to make. We can have our cake and eat it, too, in this instance. We can be skillful at dealing with people *and* have the most productive teams in our organizations.

I guess what I'm trying to say is it's safer to err on the side of assuming no one we deal with can handle direct criticism than to assume they can. Even after dealing with the same people for awhile, I'd still be careful. As a general rule, people simply don't like to be criticized, and I'd personally avoid it.

At this point, I imagine some of you are thinking: "This is just new-age hippie stuff. If someone is wrong, just tell him he is wrong and move on." I couldn't disagree more. Yes, I would say that some people seem to be able to handle blunt, direct feedback, but that's not true for everyone. I would avoid assuming everyone needs to be mature enough to handle the full-frontal assault we want to administer. It's been my experience that many people are *not* mature and will immediately take offense to our criticism. They may not outwardly show their dislike; but inside, they are feeling the sting of our words.

If you feel like you need to criticize someone else, you might want to ask yourself, "What's my motive?" Are you trying to make yourself look better, or are you trying to help the other person? No one is perfect. There are plenty of things you *could* criticize someone for, but why? What's the end game? Instead, why not look for healthy ways to encourage, edify, and correct the individual? I'll give you some tools for how to properly correct people in the next chapter.

When talking about criticism, people often like to point to individuals whose style of leadership runs contrary to what we are talking about but were successful in spite of it. I hear people throw around names like Steve Jobs and say that because he didn't operate the way we're talking about, there really is no reason they should, either. First, let me say that there is, and will only ever be, one Steve Jobs. The guy was a tech visionary and, to my understanding, did things his own way from the beginning. Modeling your leadership style after someone like him is like modeling your retirement after a lottery winner—if you think your retirement will be funded by lottery winnings, it's not going to work out for you. What *will* work out for you, from both a leadership and retirement perspective? Fundamentals. That's right, the good old fundamentals of dealing with people and the fundamentals of investing for retirement. I would never bet my retirement on winning the lottery, and I would never bet my ability to influence people on a one-in-a-million personality. Let's stick with what works for the other 99.9 percent of us. I'm not trying to put you in a box; I'm trying to help. Be a tech visionary *and* be the most caring and skilled people person on the planet.

If you want people to dislike you, criticize them—in front of others if you can. It feels like we are beating a dead horse (and grinding it into hamburger and eating it), but I really want to get the concept in this chapter across. Just don't criticize people. There are better ways to get the results we want, ways that don't create friction in our lives. I hope the goal for most people is to get better results. Stopping criticism in its tracks, in every area of our lives, will move us closer to that objective.

DO NOT GOSSIP

The second "do not" on our list is do not gossip. Just like we did with criticize, let's start out with the definition of the word to make sure we have a crystal clear understanding of what we are talking about.

> *gossip:* casual or unconstrained conversation or reports about other people, typically involving details that are not confirmed as being true

I don't think I need to provide any synonyms for this word, because it's obvious from the definition that this sort of activity is bad and should be avoided if we want to foster a healthy people environment at our workplace or church. It's written in Leviticus 19:16 (AMP), "You shall not go around as a gossip among your people, and you are not to act against the life of your neighbor [with slander or false testimony]; I am the Lord." I know this verse is from Old Testament Jewish law, but it's still useful to us as Christians living under the New Covenant because it demonstrates God's character—He doesn't approve of gossip.

Another common phrase used in place of the word "gossip" is "talking behind people's backs." I think most of us have fallen victim to this in some way, shape, or fashion, and it can be damaging to relationships. Did you like it when people were talking about you behind your back? If not, let's not do it to others. As a general rule, if we wouldn't say something to a person's face, we shouldn't say it to someone else. If the person we were talking about was standing right in front of us, would we still be saying what we are saying? We can even take it a step further. Instead of talking about an individual behind his back, why don't we go talk to him about whatever topic we feel we need to share with everyone else *except* him? Yikes, that's even scarier! Good. That should be our measuring stick as to whether we should be talking about a person behind his back.

Paul said (in Ephesians 4:29, NKJV), "Let no corrupt word proceed out of your mouth, but what is good for necessary edification, that it may impart grace to the hearers." Gossip does not edify (instruct or improve morally or intellectually) or impart grace to the hearer—it's the equivalent of verbal garbage. I talked about the power of words in chapter 11, and gossip is a powerful example of how words can bring large amounts of death to our lives and the lives of people around us. As Christians, we need to understand and apply the basics of proper communication—this is how we build a strong, healthy local church. If a church is full of people who gossip (and other harmful communication traits), there is an invisible cap on how successful it's going to be. Gossip is like a virus that slowly spreads throughout an organization. Left unchecked, it can have catastrophic effects on morale, happiness, and head count. People leave churches over gossip. People lose trust in their leaders and teammates over gossip. As Christians, gossip is something we should not tolerate and definitely not endorse or propagate. God can lead all sorts of people to a local church's front door, but if the congregation is "sick" with communication problems, many will not stick around long enough to use their skills and talents for the advancement of that church body and God's kingdom as a whole.

Picture this: You have a calling on your life to sing for God. In every measurable way, you are an extremely gifted and capable singer, leader, and songwriter. You are exactly what your new church needs (they've been praying for a person just like you), and you feel like you were led to be there. After attending for a couple of weeks, you decide to contact the worship leader and tell her that you'd like to sit in on some rehearsals because you're interested in joining the team later down the road. That next Tuesday, when rehearsal is held, you arrive and begin visiting with members of the worship team. You notice that people don't seem happy. You overhear a conversation tearing down the leader.

One person is talking about how she saw another member of the team at the mall wearing a shirt that was way too tight. Another person says he thinks the drummer might have a drinking problem. Would you want to join this team? No way—you'd be walking into a minefield! At the very least, it would make the decision to join more difficult.

There are people in your congregation right now who are the answer to your prayers. You need an amazing children's director? That person might already be in your church. What is he waiting for? He is watching. He is observing people to decide if he wants to get involved or not. Even if he believes God is calling him, he may not be mature enough to just follow the leading. The worse our skill with people (with things like rampant gossip), the more reasons we give those people to not join the team and use their God-given gifts within our churches. God can lead them to us, and we can absolutely turn them off by disregarding the fundamentals of interpersonal communication.

This same principle applies to businesses, too! You may need a qualified individual for an important position, and the unhealthy people environment in your organization can drive applicants away. Highly qualified people realize they are in demand and don't have to stick around a company that is a drain on them emotionally. A hefty salary will only work for so long before people get sick and tired of the dysfunction and leave.

Gossip doesn't only involve information about others that we don't know is true. Even if we know something to be absolutely true, and we share that information with someone else, we're spreading gossip. The information we want to share may be damaging to an individual and our organization. Is it worth it? Now you might be saying, "Well, Tony, other people need to know what that person did." I would recommend you tread with caution here. Do other people *really* need to know about it, or are you just looking for the fix you get from sharing a tasty morsel of information? If the safety of others is involved, then yes, I would absolutely share the information. It's been my experience, however, that very little information falls into this category. Even if something is big enough that it can't be ignored, we can be selective about whom we share it with in order to get the situation resolved properly. For instance, if you happen to see the married youth pastor leaving a local liquor store with a bottle of whiskey in one hand and kissing a strange woman, the right thing to do would be to ask him about it first. If he admits it was him, then maybe your next step is to meet with the senior pastor to discuss the issue. Give your pastor a chance to deal with it—that's his job. The wrong thing to do would be to immediately contact everyone you know and share what you saw. That's damaging to the church and damaging to *your* character. You do not want to be known as a gossip.

Some people think that they have no choice in the matter and they *have to* comment on what they have seen or heard. This is totally false! A person can ask what we think about so-and-so, and we can say we don't have an opinion—at least not one we're going to voice. How many people do that? As Christians, we should use wisdom to know when to speak and when to hold our tongues. Nothing says we have to give our opinions about another person's life or spread information that we've seen or heard, especially if we know it could be damaging to the person we are talking about.

When we choose to gossip, we lose people's trust. Why? Because we've just *shown* them, by gossiping about another person, that we will talk about them behind their backs if we get half a chance, too. We've just demonstrated by our actions that we would have no problem gossiping about them—because we're doing it right now! The side effect of this is that people will trust us less and share less information with us. Less trust means less influence with people. Gossip can be limiting opportunities in our lives. Choose not to gossip.

Gossip also gives "legs" to an issue and causes it to live longer than it should. If and when the person we're gossiping about rises above the issue, most people aren't there to see it—they don't get the good report along with the bad. Forevermore, that person is now viewed in a bad light because we chose to talk about how he or she messed up. How fair is that? People are really good about sharing the negative; but since the good isn't as exciting, they rarely go around to everyone they've talked to and report that the person has fixed the problem and is now doing OK. Gossip doesn't seem to work that way for some reason.

Don't be a mouthpiece for the enemy. Don't do his work for him. He knows how damaging gossip is to the church or your organization. Don't give in to the temptation to gossip. It's one of the primary ways he sows strife into the church. Do what James said (in James 4:7, NKJV) instead: "Therefore submit to God. Resist the devil and he will flee from you." Resist the temptation to gossip. You can do it! Instead, say: "I am not a gossip. These words would not edify or bring grace to a listener, therefore I will not say them." You're in control of your mouth, not anyone else.

DO NOT COMPLAIN

The last "do not" on our list is do not complain. Once again, let's start out with the definition, so we all can agree on what we are talking about.

> *complain:* express dissatisfaction or annoyance about a state of affairs or an event

Some synonyms of complain are grumble and whine. We can see why this is an undesirable way to conduct ourselves!

In Philippians 2:14–15 (NKJV), we are instructed to "Do all things without complaining and disputing, that you may become blameless and harmless, children of God without fault in the midst of a crooked and perverse generation, among whom you shine as lights in the world." Right there, in black and white, Paul said to do all things without complaining and disputing (without bad-tempered discontent, without murmurings; the moral, the intellectual rebellion against God). If we do that, we will be blameless and harmless, and shine as lights in the world. Something else we get out of this verse is that apparently if we complain and dispute, we will be blameful and harmful (the opposite of blameless and harmless)—and we won't shine as lights in the world. If we want to stand out as Christians, one of the easiest ways to do that is to choose not to complain.

From a practical standpoint, people don't like being around complainers. These are people who constantly are focused on the negative in any situation and make sure everyone else knows about it, too. They seem to *find* something to complain about just to strike up a conversation. They suck the life out of everyone around them and sometimes are actively avoided for that reason.

Complaining adds no value whatsoever to any interaction, so it should be avoided altogether. Instead of complaining, why not use our words to sow into the people around us? If you're like me, the people I admire the most are not complainers—they are problem solvers and overcomers. If a situation isn't right, they find a way to fix it. If they can't fix it, they figure out what they *can* do and focus on that instead. Because of that, I like them, and they have more influence with me. We should endeavor to be like that ourselves. The negative always is going to be around—that's unavoidable. What we can control is how we respond to it and what we choose to focus on.

It's good to remember that if we are being led by God, and we are complaining about our circumstances, we are actually complaining about God's direction for our lives. I don't know about you, but I *do not* want to do that. The Israelites did this very thing when they journeyed out of Egypt. After being in the wilderness for a couple of months, they thought they were complaining about their situation against Moses and Aaron (Exodus 16:2), but they actually were complaining against the Lord (Exodus 16:7). He noticed, too. (Gulp!)

Complaining is a drag on everyone involved. If your team is in the middle of a "rough patch," everyone already knows. People aren't interested in being beat over the head with a bunch of complaints. What they *are* interested in is how they are going to change their current situation and get back on track. This is accomplished by developing a plan, executing on the plan, and course-correcting along the way—*not* by complaining. People admire others who can stay positive in the midst of any situation. If you are this kind of person, you have a positive influence on the people around you, which is the entire purpose of this book!

Paul said (in Philippians 4:11–13, NKJV): "Not that I speak in regard to need, for I have learned in whatever state I am, to be content: I know how to be abased, and I know how to abound. Everywhere and in all things I have learned both to be full and to be hungry, both to abound and to suffer need. I can do all things through Christ who strengthens me." Paul *learned* to be content in Christ regardless of his situation. We can learn to be the same way because the same Spirit who was in Paul is in us if we are born again. The more we learn about our new nature in Jesus, the less we find we have to complain about.

14

How to Correct People

At some point in your life, you're going to run into a situation where you have to correct someone. It's unavoidable and should be looked at as an opportunity to sow into that person's life, instead of something you'd rather avoid altogether. After all, you are helping that person to change his or her behavior in order to get better results—how can that be a bad thing? I think where many people get tripped up is they feel uncomfortable confronting others, because they don't have a game plan for how they'd go about doing it—they lack options. I'm about ready to give you some more tools to add to your tool belt, so the next time you have to correct someone, you can meet the challenge with confidence and enthusiasm.

The strategies I'm about to outline can be used on anyone in your life—friends, co-workers, and family. Just because you have kids doesn't mean you're exempt from treating them with respect, too. I know it can be tough as a parent because our kids seem to know all of the right buttons to push with us. Don't let that stop you from doing what's right. If they don't learn these behaviors from you, where are they going to pick them up? I'm convinced that if we can do the things in this book with our families, we can do them with *anyone*. Use your family members as your test subjects.

DOES IT MATTER IF THEY ARE WRONG?

The very first thing we should ask ourselves if we think we need to correct someone is this: Does it really matter if the person is wrong? I mean, does it *really* matter? Is something important at stake if someone doesn't correct the individual? In my estimation, this is rarely the case. Many times, people act like the self-proclaimed "word police" and feel it's their duty to correct every syllable of every word that comes out of someone's mouth. There also are "fact-checkers" who have to make sure every single word is 100-percent, verifiably true—and if it's not, they'll be sure to let you know. People do not like this, and if we operate this way, we are losing influence with them.

Dave Hendricksen, author of the book *12 Essential Skills for Software Architects*, said, "One of the first principles to learn in becoming a gracious professional is to choose relationships over correctness." This is a powerful statement and one that has stuck with me ever since I first read his book years ago. Is it more important to correct a person or to keep his or her goodwill? Depending on how we go about administering the correction, we could be making large withdrawals out of our bank account with that individual and possibly risk going in the red. So ask yourself, "Is it more important that I correct this person or that I maintain a strong relationship with the individual?"

Working in the technology industry, I always run up against people who are overly hung up on the details. Every statement has to be absolutely correct, or we have to spend ten minutes hammering that out before we can move on. Yes, there is a time and a place for detailed discussion, but being overly detailed across the board slows down progress and is not necessary, especially in strategic conversations. Many times, it's sufficient to be generally correct in order to move the discussion along.

Personally speaking, when certain people I've worked with were present at a meeting, I stopped participating—I got tired of having to defend every word and idea that came out of my mouth. These kinds of people shut down creativity, because no one wants to have their ideas put through the ringer in front of everyone else. Bad ideas have a way of getting weeded out through the normal process. Let's control them on the back end, where we'll put more rigor around each idea, rather than the front end, where we are more interested in collecting as many ideas as possible. The more people you have who are wholeheartedly participating in your organization, the more successful it's going to be. Don't let someone put a damper on that by being overly critical at the wrong time.

Our goal should be to create the safest, most supportive atmosphere we can within our team. If we constantly are correcting everyone's words and statements, it makes people want to avoid us. It also makes them feel bad about themselves. Now, instead of brainstorming with us on a possible solution to a problem, they are more concerned with speaking perfectly, which significantly limits the quality of thinking we're getting out of them. If we want the best out of people, they need to feel safe around us.

I occasionally lead brainstorming sessions as part of my job. When I lead these sessions, the first idea I like to write on the whiteboard is "time machine." I do this to let everyone know that anything short of traveling back and forth in time is an acceptable idea. I personally think it lightens the mood in the room and lets people know they are in a safe environment. People typically will offer their ideas least likely to be rejected first. If you show them they're in a safe environment, and there aren't any "sharks in the water" (people waiting to attack their ideas), they'll start to bring out their really good ideas—the ideas that might transform your business or volunteer organization.

CORRECT PEOPLE IN PRIVATE, IF POSSIBLE

If you find yourself in a situation where you do need to correct someone, the best way to do it is in private. No one likes to have his or her faults or shortcomings paraded out in front of everyone to see. Making corrections in private allows people to save face among their fellow co-workers and will take some of the inevitable defensiveness out of the air because they don't have to stand up for themselves to the degree that they would around a bunch of other people. Correcting people in private should be viewed as a common courtesy.

People are social creatures and anything that threatens their social standing will be viewed as an attack, especially if we don't have very strong relationships with them to begin with. This is another reason why building up large bank accounts with the people in our lives can be so helpful—it protects us in cases where we do have to administer correction in front of an audience. To the best of your ability, try to take the topic "offline" and discuss it in private. Follow the Golden Rule, and you should be safe the majority of the time.

Listen, I don't live in a fairy tale land where every situation can be planned for ahead of time. Sometimes we have to make it up as we go along. What I'm trying to do is provide a solid framework that works in the majority of the cases. I acknowledge that there are some instances where we have to correct someone in a public setting, and it's unavoidable. In situations like this, be mindful of the other person and frame up the correction in the best way possible.

Let's say you are in a meeting room with six other people. You are on a conference call with a supplier who needs the numbers to place an order for some materials you need. When the supplier asks how much to order for you, one of your key employees, Sarah, boldly answers with the wrong number! What do you do? Well, for starters, one thing you could do is tell your supplier you're going to put the call on mute for a minute while you discuss the topic further with your team—this will minimize the audience. You could then start asking Sarah questions to lead her to where her error is—even if you *know* the correct answer. She'll probably still feel a little embarrassed that she was wrong, but the way you handled it minimizes the embarrassment and allows *her* to find her own mistake. See how this looks in real life? Tactics like this are what can separate us from everyone else. Little by little, we can gain more influence with our teams and the people around us.

Sometimes it can be helpful to think of life like a marathon rather than a sprint. In our quest to be fast, thorough, and impressive to our superiors (by sprinting), are we affecting our performance later in the race? Sure, at mile two we may be looking really good, but what about at mile twenty? Will we still have as much goodwill and influence with the people around us, or will we have spent all of it in our quest to stand out using selfish tactics? Decide to correct people in a way that not only works for you in the short term but also ensures you're in a good position toward the end of the race, too.

FOCUS ON THE BEHAVIOR, NOT THE PERSON

People will receive our correction much better if we keep it impersonal. Always make sure to focus on the behavior that's not meeting the standard, instead of the person. If we focus on the person, our correction will be more damaging because it is a direct blow against the individual. Correction should never be a personal attack.

If you've ever served in a leadership position at your church, you've most likely had to correct someone. When I played guitar for my local church, we had three teams of musicians, and I was the leader of one of the teams. When we met and rehearsed music, there were endless opportunities to put this principle into practice.

One of my major responsibilities was to make sure the music we played sounded the best it could—as professional as possible. This required a fair amount of public correction on my part to make sure we played the songs correctly and we all sounded good together. (Remember, I told you there would be times when public correction is unavoidable.) That was just the nature of the setting. It wasn't feasible to pull people aside, in private, to address execution issues during practice. This would have taken way too long, and other players needed to hear the correction so they could apply it to their own instruments, if applicable. I had to get really good at helping some people with other people present.

If something didn't sound right while we practiced a song, I'd wait for the song to finish (or stop it right then, if it warranted it) and then start asking questions (more on this in the next chapter) to lead us to the problem. I would say something like, "I'm not sure that part during the verse sounded right, what do you think?" Do you see how this is different than, "*You* played that part wrong"? The first correction is focused on the part being played. The second correction is focused on the individual. The difference may seem subtle to you, but it means a lot to the person receiving the correction, especially in front of other people.

If you are reading this and you're a worship leader at a church, I recommend getting *really* good at the principles in this book. Musicians are an interesting breed of people, and it takes special care to guide and grow them without offending them or wounding their creative spirit. For some of these people, their art is sacred to them and they view it as an extension of themselves. In order to get the best out of our people, we need to become smooth as butter at correcting and guiding them. Jesus said (in Luke 16:10, NKJV), "He who is faithful in a very little thing is faithful also in much; and he who is unrighteous in a very little thing is unrighteous also in much." Being a good steward (Matthew 25:14–30) and being faithful with the people you have now will allow God to increase the size and influence of your ministry.

CUSHION THE BLOW

> *A soft answer turns away wrath, but a harsh word stirs up anger.*
> *—Proverbs 15:1 (NKJV)*

This is never more true than when it comes to correcting people. The key to getting the results we want, while keeping the goodwill of the person we're correcting, is all about our approach—a soft answer. What I'm going to give you right now are a couple of concrete tools that you can use to cushion the blow when you find you have to correct someone.

Hopefully at this point, you've already pulled the person aside and created a safe environment to administer the correction. Ideally, you already would have a healthy bank account with the person, but even if you don't, the strategies I'm about to share still will be effective. Don't go into a discussion like this unprepared! Know, in general, what you plan to say and what tools you plan to apply. There is absolutely no reason to fly by the seat of your pants and awkwardly stumble through the conversation, which would make it even more uncomfortable than it already might be for you.

The "sandwich method" is a popular approach to administering correction. (See how Jesus used this approach as He addressed the churches in Revelation 2–3.) The idea here is that you start and end with something positive and sandwich the correction in between the two. The positive remarks do not have to be over-the-top and definitely should not be any form of flattery (excessive and insincere praise). We are just talking about a little something to make it easier on the person. If you were going to perform surgery on someone, you'd give the patient some painkillers first, right? All we're trying to do here is numb the pain a little before we pull out our scalpel and go to work.

Some have expressed concern that using this method would mask the real issue, so a person would receive the positive remarks but miss the correction. I don't think I've ever seen it work out this way, but perhaps we could be so overly positive with the ends of the sandwich that the person doesn't think anything needs to change. Starting and ending with something positive should not be a thirty-minute-long exposition on how the individual is a credit to humanity and that anyone with half a brain would be *lucky* to have him or her working on his team. Just use something short and sweet to help dull the upcoming pain. Start out by saying you were impressed with the work he did on project X (if it's true). Or, say something about how you appreciate her always being on time (if she is). We should never lie, and we should keep it to a reasonable length.

Always use wisdom when dealing with people. We are not talking about applying an unchangeable rule here. If you find a person isn't responding to your method of correction as it is, try adjusting your approach. We all are growing in these things. If you find something doesn't work for you, just tweak it a little the next time around. You get better at influencing people the more you do it. Don't give up on the idea just because you tried it once, and it didn't work. Maybe you just need a little more practice.

Another approach that can be effective at cushioning the blow when you are correcting people is to start out by talking about your own personal struggles. This communicates to people that you are authentic. You know you're not perfect, and you don't expect others to be perfect, either. Everybody makes mistakes sometimes. The goal, of course, is to make fewer and fewer mistakes, but when someone is starting out, he or she is going to need a lot of correction. Even seasoned vets occasionally make mistakes, and starting out with a personal struggle still can be effective. Ideally, we'd like to be able to share about a similar issue in our past that we struggled with, but that's not mandatory. A simple statement like, "When I first started, I had a difficult time doing X" can do wonders for taking some of the defensiveness out of the air. When we make an effort to relate to a person, it can help separate the behavior that's being corrected from the person receiving the correction.

Don't assume everyone is like you. I've run into people who just want others to give it to them straight. That might be fine for you, but realize the people on your team are not you! It's safer to assume everyone could be offended and then change your approach after you get to know individuals better. If we take the bull-in-a-China-shop approach, we might create even more problems for ourselves down the road.

As we end this chapter, let's review three strategies we now can use when correcting people: (1) Correct people in private, if possible; (2) Focus on the behavior, not the person; and (3) Cushion the blow. From now on, when we need to administer correction, we can affect how well the correction will be received and how much goodwill we will keep after the correction is over. I hope you can see there is a *huge* difference between public confrontation and ridicule, or pulling someone aside and using the sandwich method on them. There's no comparison! The first approach *will* come back to haunt you. Creating the best place to work is all about placing importance on doing the day-to-day tasks of human interaction effectively.

15

The Power of a Question

People don't like being told what to do. So, instead of issuing direct orders to people, ask them questions. This simple concept is one of my top five favorites from this part of the book, and it has radically changed my daily interactions with people. Even if I already have thought out the direction we should take in a particular situation, I'll pose questions to lead others to the same conclusion. The effects have been amazing! You can transform yourself from that "jerk who tells everyone what he should do" to a people influencer who guides individuals to the best solution. In addition to promoting internal team harmony, you might be pleasantly surprised how many people have *better* ideas than you! As leaders, we never want to assume that we always know the correct way to handle a situation. There's value in listening to others' input—maybe we'll hear something we hadn't thought of.

The higher you go in an organization, whether business or volunteer, the bigger an impact your simple questions can have on people, too. Can you imagine how honored someone on the usher's team would be if you, the pastor of your church, asked him how he would solve a problem the church is currently facing? The person would think, "Man, the pastor thinks highly enough of me to ask my opinion!" It's huge! Never underestimate the power of simple questions; they can have a profound effect on people.

INCLUDE PEOPLE IN THE SOLUTION

Asking questions includes people in the solution to a problem. When you include people in the solution, they now own a little piece of it, which makes all the difference in the world. As a leader, are you wondering how to get more involvement and commitment out of your people? Well, for starters, are you having them help you to design the solutions to issues your organization faces? If you are the type of person who likes to tell others what to do, it is not *their* solution they are implementing, it's *your* solution. Do you see the difference? If the solution fails, *your* solution failed, not theirs—they never had true ownership of any piece of it. If you don't involve your people in the decision-making process, you'll have no real commitment from them. Sure, you may have people implementing your ideas, but you don't get that true, "sold out" buy-in that leaders say they are looking for. Why? Because there is no ownership on the part of the people who are doing the work. If we just want people to obey our orders, we shouldn't be surprised when we end up leading a team of one—ourselves!

When people are involved in identifying a solution, they give an extra effort because their reputation is on the line just as yours is. They don't want to have to say, "I was wrong" when they helped design the solution, so they will work extra hard to make sure it succeeds. This is not just a principle for corporate America—it applies to churches and volunteer organizations, as well.

Consider this scenario: You decide you're going to roll out a new program at your church. The program needs about twenty people to make it work, but you figure you'll just find the bodies you need by putting up a slide at the beginning of service. You design the entire program, decide how it's going to operate, and the last thing you need are the people. How do you think this is going to work out for you? You *might* get enough people to respond, but they won't be nearly as engaged as they would have been if you got them on board first and *then* designed the program with their help. If you design it with them, you get more commitment and effort from them—that's just the way people operate. Think about it. If you create a piece of the solution, you almost feel morally obligated to see that it succeeds because it's yours! I haven't met very many people who want *their* ideas to fail. It becomes personal at that point, and that makes all the difference in the world.

Anything that requires a lot of time and energy on the part of the team members is especially susceptible to what we are talking about here. If all you need are twenty people to pick up trash for an hour at the church, maybe you don't need to get together and hear everyone's ideas—or perhaps you just do it real quick right before you start. However, if you are leading a project that requires more out of people than just showing up, you'd be missing one of the best ways to keep people plugged in and motivated, if you don't ask them for their input. People want their voices to be heard, especially when you want something significant from them. If we ignore this principle, we shouldn't be surprised when people aren't as engaged as we'd like.

Asking questions almost completely liberates you from having to be the bad guy. Instead of always having to be the person who decides something isn't possible, you can lead the team to that solution by asking questions, so they can see why the decision is made a particular way. Then, in the cases when the team is pressured for time, and you have to make a quick judgment call, you have at least built up your bank account with those around you to support the quick decision. You might be thinking, "But isn't that just a big waste of time?" Well, it depends on how much you value the long-term goodwill of the people around you. Remember, too, that it's not just about getting the most efficient solution decided at the moment—it's about long-term influence with people. You could be known as a person whom people want on their team. People could seek you out for advice. From a Christian standpoint, this is huge! The more influence we carry with people, the more opportunities we are going to have to minister to them—not only from a work perspective but also from a spiritual one. You never know what conversations you may strike up later because a person likes you and likes being around you. You might end up leading him or her to the Lord at a coffeehouse after work.

Using questions to lead people where you want them to go is a great way to foster an atmosphere of inclusion in your organization. Questions put others in the driver's seat and give them an opportunity to voice their opinions and say what *they* would do if they were the ones making the final decision. Instead of just following orders, now you're making them think about what they're doing. This grows leaders. It also makes people feel important and is just another small way we can gain influence with others and strengthen our relationships with them.

16

Appreciate People and Make Them Feel Important

People are chronically underappreciated—at work, at church, at home, at you name it! Because of this, the rare individuals who take it upon themselves to liberally appreciate people in their lives have a *huge* advantage over others. As we pointed out in an earlier chapter, people tend to be self-focused, which causes them to miss countless opportunities every day to sow into the lives of the people around them. Being more appreciative of the people around us can radically change our relationships, especially if we don't do much of it right now.

If we take people for granted long enough, we eventually will encounter problems. Continual withdrawals from their bank accounts only can happen for so long before they become overdrawn. Making people feel important and appreciating them are ways we can continually make deposits into their accounts. We literally can make every interaction with a person into a deposit. We can get work done *and* deposit into others' accounts at the same time. People want to be around individuals who operate this way. Be like this, and you might be surprised how many people will want to hang around you. You will be recharging their batteries, and it won't take that much effort on your part.

APPRECIATION MOTIVATES PEOPLE

If you are not consciously appreciating the people around you, you're missing out on one of the simplest and least expensive ways to motivate people there is. In most cases, appreciation is free (we'll talk about some exceptions later) and is quick to administer. A simple "Great job cleaning the bathrooms—you clean the mirrors better than anyone else" can do wonders for the morale of an individual. Make sure you are sincere when appreciating others, but that shouldn't be hard, because people do all sorts of good things all day long.

Consider also how you can be specific with your appreciation. If a person did a good job creating slides for the service at church, tell him or her specifically what you liked about them—it makes it more personal. Think about it. What would you rather hear your daughter say, "Good job on that whole mom thing," or "Mom, I really like the way you do my ponytails—you're good at it, because they don't fall out toward the end of the day"? Calling out something specific someone has done is much more effective than throwing out a blanket "Good job" as you pass by.

I see these sorts of "blanket appreciations" all the time in the workplace. E-mail can be the worst for this because managers seem to think if they send out a "Great job, team!" to everyone in the company that it actually makes people feel appreciated. It doesn't. Their hearts might be in the right place, but specific appreciation—ideally one-on-one—comes across as more genuine and is the best way to acknowledge something someone has done.

No one likes to work tirelessly, year after year, and never receive any recognition—no one! Even Christians, who are supposed to be more selfless than unbelievers, need to hear words of appreciation and encouragement on a consistent basis—it's food for our soul. Don't "starve" the people around you by never appreciating them.

Husbands, when is the last time you appreciated your wives? Think about it. When is the last time you sincerely thanked your wife for the good things she's doing for you and your family? Even if she's far from perfect, she still does a lot of praiseworthy things. Is she patient with the kids? Appreciate her for it. Is she really good at managing the finances of the family? Appreciate her for it. Pick some things she does well and appreciate her for them. She needs this from you, and no one else can replace the type of appreciation you can give.

Underappreciated wives are a time bomb waiting to explode. It's very hard for a person to just give, give, give all day long and have no one even acknowledge it. And if you're not appreciated, either, be the person to sow that first seed into your spouse. Someone has to get the ship moving in the right direction—it may as well be you. Appreciate your wife more, and things will just start working better for the whole family.

If you are in a high-level position of authority in your organization, *do not* underestimate the power that your appreciation can have on motivating the people under you, especially the ones "tending to the fields," as I like to say. If you're a CEO or pastor, consider how you may be missing out daily on the ability to change lives with simple words of appreciation. Whether you like it or not, people have put you on a pedestal and give a lot of weight to what you say. If you talk to them about something praiseworthy that they are doing for your organization, you validate them as a person, and *everybody* likes that.

Most appreciation we ever give will cost us nothing, so what are we waiting for? We already know people are figuratively starving for it, so why not hand it out as fast and as often as possible? Deciding to honestly and frequently appreciate people is sort of like providing a food aid program to a starving country. People are starving for what we have. But the difference between us and a relief program is that we'll never run out of "food"—we can just keep on giving and giving! We know people want it. We know we have it. Why not use the power of appreciation to sow into lives and motivate people to do bigger and better things? It *will* come back to us—we already learned that.

APPRECIATION SHOULD BE A LIFESTYLE

While occasionally appreciating people and making them feel important is a good start, the goal is to make these activities a habit that becomes a part of our everyday lives. Similar to lifting weights, if we want true, long-lasting change, we have to hit the gym more than just a couple of times a year. When it comes to forming good habits, we'll probably have to continually remind ourselves to do the right things at first; but after a few short weeks, we'll start doing them without thinking.

Mary Kay Ash, founder of Mary Kay Cosmetics, said, "Everyone has an invisible sign hanging from his neck saying, 'Make me feel important.'" Everyone wants to feel like he is doing something that matters. Everyone wants to feel loved and connected to something larger than himself. One way to help people feel connected is to help them feel important, because they are important.

There is nothing more exquisitely made on all the earth than us. Every person you meet is a living masterpiece—a completely unique creation with a specific call of God on his or her life. If we recognize this, then treating people like they are important gets a whole lot easier. People are *extremely* important to God! We should treat them the same way He does.

As Christians, a culture of appreciation should be at the core of our churches and businesses. Compared to eternity, we live short lives on the earth; so why not make the most of our lives while we are here? Why waste any time taking people for granted and ignoring their contributions when it takes so little to connect with them on a personal level through appreciation? We should be setting the standard for how organizations run, because we have God on our side. We've been born again and have the Holy Spirit to guide us. We have so many amazing promises available to us in the New Covenant that it's almost unfair. Let's spread some of that thankfulness and joy by calling out people for the great things they do and helping them to do even greater things. Words of encouragement can change people's lives.

If you're the type of person who doesn't regularly appreciate the people around you, you're missing out on a huge opportunity. I know, it may feel uncomfortable interacting with people on a personal level, but you're going to have to make a decision. Do you want the results of appreciation in your organization or not? Do you want happier, better connected people or not? Wanting those results without doing anything to get them means you're not going to have them. I have an easy solution to help you: Make yourself appreciate people. Put systems in place that you can follow to make sure you are doing the things you know you should be doing. Work with a buddy to help each other grow in this area. Put reminders in your phone or e-mail calendar. A simple calendar reminder like "Go appreciate someone on my team at 3:00" is an easy and effective way to force yourself to do what you already know is right. After you start seeing the results, you'll become more motivated to keep up with it—without needing all of the extra help.

TANGIBLE GIFTS

Let's be honest here. Would you rather hear someone say that you've done a good job, or come back to your workspace and find a handwritten note of appreciation attached to your favorite snack (candy, drink, etc.)? I don't know about you, but I prefer the latter. People, in general, really like getting gifts from others regardless of age, income bracket, or gender. Use this knowledge of human nature to help build out your Opportunity Tree more quickly and to recognize the contributions of the people around you.

Tangible gifts mean a lot more to people because someone has to spend time and/or money to put them together. In a money-obsessed world, where everyone seems to try to horde as much of it as possible, the person who actively finds ways to give it away instantly separates himself or herself from everyone else. How many people give you tangible gifts as a form of appreciation? Probably not that many, if you're in line with the average person. What this means is we can instantly operate at a higher level than most people, which gives us an advantage as we attempt to become more influential with the people around us. This is just another way we can express the love of God in us. Operating in this way makes us attractive to unbelievers, which increases our ability to positively influence them from a spiritual standpoint.

It's written in Proverbs 18:16 (AMP), "A man's gift [given in love or courtesy] makes room for him and brings him before great men." Thousands of years ago, Solomon recognized that our gifts open up opportunities in our lives. We can use this principle to make room for us in the lives of the people around us. Someone might be asking,

"Wouldn't I just be bribing the people around me?" Only you can answer that question for yourself. What's in your heart when you give the gift? Speaking for myself, I want to appreciate people for *their* benefit, but I'm also aware of what the gift is going to do for me. It's just another form of sowing and reaping.

We are told (in Acts 20:35, NKJV) that Jesus said, "It is more blessed to give than to receive." Receiving is blessed, but giving is even more blessed! Anyone who has given with pure motives can attest to this—it made you feel awesome! Tangible gifts of appreciation are good for both the giver and the receiver. Don't miss out on this easy way to make both of your lives better.

I could tell you what's most important to you. Do you want to know how? I'd just follow you around for a week and see what you spend your time and money on. If you say you truly value people but don't spend your time or money helping them, appreciating them, or making them feel important, then you're lying to yourself. That would be like saying golf is the most important thing to you, but you don't own a set of golf clubs and haven't golfed in the past ten years. Sure, maybe it used to be important to you, but it isn't anymore. I know this may be difficult for some people to hear, but I'm trying to help you to see a potential problem, so you can fix it. Do not be deceived! If you don't spend any time or money on something (an activity, organization, person, etc.), then it's not that important to you. Sure, you can acknowledge the importance *of* it, but unless you're personally invested in it via time or money, it isn't that important to *you*. We will call this the "Universal Importance Test," or UIT for short.

In Matthew 6:21 (NKJV), Jesus said it perfectly, "For where your treasure is, there your heart will be also." If all of your money is tied up in the stock market, the stock market all of a sudden becomes *very* important to you. If you spend all of your money on your car, your car now is very important to you. Is the local homeless shelter *that* important to you if you never volunteer there or donate resources to it? Nope. If you never spend time appreciating people, developing them, making them feel important, or giving to them, are they really that important to you? According to the UIT, they aren't.

INITIATE INTERACTIONS WITH PEOPLE

I can sense introverts squirming in their seats right now because we are going to talk about why we should proactively seek opportunities to interact with people in order to build stronger relationships. In a later chapter, I'll give you some tips on how to be a better conversationalist; but right now, I'll try to get you to see the importance of getting out of your seat and getting to know people better.

Initiating interactions with people around us makes them feel important, especially if you are in any position of leadership at your business or church. Remember what we just talked about? People know that you have limited time and resources, so when you spend some of it with them, it *shows* them that they are important to you. Remember, if your words and your actions disagree, people will always believe your actions. You can say people are important, but if you never talk to them and get to know them, the message you're sending is, "You're important, just not *that* important."

When I talk with people in leadership positions, I encourage them to *make* time to get out and talk with people. Do you realize, for a pastor of a church, if you set aside just thirty minutes each week to contact a single church member, you could talk to more than fifty people in a single year? For some pastors, this would be a good chunk of their church! If you have a larger church, you might be thinking "That's only a small amount of the congregation—so what?" It's fifty real, breathing people whom you could bless by connecting with them on a deeper level. It shouldn't be a time thing; it should be an importance thing.

You can get as creative as you want to in this space. Hold a get-together where you invite a dozen people to the church for ice cream once a week. The issue isn't really what you're doing as a group, just that you connect with individuals to deposit into their bank accounts.

The only way to significantly build stronger relationships with people is by spending time with them. There is no other way. If you doubt this, why don't you try moving to a different city and tell me how the relationships with your current friends and family fare? At best, they'll stagnate. What typically happens is they deteriorate because you're not spending the necessary time with each other anymore. This is why long-distance relationships seldom work out—people begin growing roots in a new location and feel closer to those directly around them. No amount of e-mailing or texting can make up for this physical separation.

Do you feel disconnected at work? Start spending more time with your co-workers. If you do this, you naturally will start feeling more connected to them. Do you feel anxiety because your church is growing, and you prefer a smaller setting on Sunday? This is an easy fix: Get to know the new people better. I realize you might not be able to know everybody, but the more people you do know, the more connected you will feel to the church. You have a part to play in how connected you are to anything or anybody. If you feel like an outsider looking in, kick down the imaginary door and get inside!

Initiating interactions with other people comes easier for some of us, but all of us can get better at it. Don't think you're not good with people. All you need is a little practice and some go-to tools to help you in situations that typically would make you feel uncomfortable. People make the world go 'round. The better we get at interacting with others, the more successful we will be at anything we put our hands to. If you have problems connecting with others, keep reading, and I'll try to help you. What I'm hoping you will recognize is that you *can* get better with people, and it is in your best interest (and God's—remember you two are a team) to do so.

Don't limit yourself in life because of fear—live by God's kind of faith. Fear puts you in a box. Faith in God and His promises to us removes barriers and changes circumstances in our lives. We're going to have to step outside of our comfort zone and be the ones to initiate interactions with others. We are going to need to be the ones who approach other people and say words of encouragement or recognize a contribution they've made. Appreciation never expressed is not appreciation at all.

17

Get to Know Others

One of the primary ways to get along better with people is to get to know them on a personal level. How many times have you met a person whom, on first impression, you didn't particularly care for, but later you ended up being friends with? This has happened to me several times over the past few years. What was the breakthrough in each relationship? Spending some time together and getting to know more about the person.

It's been my experience that some people create a shell around them to protect themselves from others. Maybe they've been hurt in the past, or maybe they are just naturally more standoffish. On the surface, they seem cold and aloof; but in actuality, they are nice, funny, and loving people—you just have to spend a little extra effort penetrating that shell and showing them you aren't a threat.

There is this one fellow I worked with, "Ron." On the surface, Ron was 100 percent business as usual. He didn't go out of his way to talk with people, and he put off a sort of leave-me-alone kind of vibe. He was a fantastic employee, he just didn't possess one of those bubbly sorts of personalities. I decided to make it my personal goal to get to know him a little better because I've found these types of people often become some of my most rewarding relationships.

Over the course of several months, I took every opportunity to find out more about Ron. I found out he served in the military—so did I! We instantly bonded over that common experience. I found out that he is a huge fan of music—so am I! We started to share different bands with each other that we thought the other person would like. What was the outcome of all of this? He turned out to be one of my favorite people at work. He's funny, interesting, and a joy to be around. He's great! Had I not taken the time to get to know him, I would have missed out on a relationship that has increased my quality of life. More, and better, relationships make us happier people.

WHAT'S IMPORTANT TO THEM?

When getting to know more about people, remember the goal is to find out more about *them*, not to cram everything about you down their throats. As a general rule, people are their own favorite topic and are most interested in talking about themselves and what they like—let them do that. Find out what they are passionate about and talk about that. You may end up talking about work-related topics at first, but the eventual goal is to connect with others on a deeper level—anyone can talk to them about work, but you care about them more than that and want to know what they *really* like to do.

It's completely acceptable to ask others about someone else with the intent of finding out more about that person, too. You can then use this information to kick-start some of your conversations later down the road. For example, if you're trying to get to know someone on the team you just joined, it might be a good idea to ask your manager or a co-worker what kinds of activities the person likes. If you find out your team member likes to mountain bike, you can use this information when you strike up a conversation with him or her in the future. It looks something like: "I heard you like to mountain bike. Can you suggest a trail for a novice like me?" See how easy that was? And if he or she is like most people, the person will go on and on about the topic because it's something the individual genuinely likes.

People feel connected to those whom they feel understand them on a deeper level than the average person. If we take the time to get to know others in a more meaningful way than the occasional "Hey" as we walk past each other, we'll expand our ability to positively influence them. This connection is important from a Christian standpoint because it can open the door to helping others experience more of God in their lives, especially if we've been consistently conducting ourselves in a godly way. Talking about God with someone we have a connection with is completely different than talking about God with a stranger. In the latter, the stranger may be unsure of our motives; whereas in the former, he knows us personally and typically will give more weight to the things we say.

MAKE YOURSELF AVAILABLE

If you look like you don't want to talk to people, people will avoid interacting with you. If you never go to where the people are, you will miss out on opportunities to get to know them better. You can't hole up in your office all day long and expect to have any sort of deeper connection with people—that's just wishful thinking. Even if you're someone who's paid by the hour, there are opportunities available to you to get to know those around you better. Make it a point to interact with others—not just for your sake but for theirs, as well. People want to be connected to others in their organization. It makes them feel happier and safer.

Many businesses have common areas where employees tend to linger. When I was younger and worked at McDonald's, we had a break room. At my current workplace, the common area is where the coffee machines are. People from all over the floor come here to get snacks, heat up their lunches, and most importantly—get coffee! Places like this are ideal spots to connect with people we may not normally interact with—kind of like the watering hole in a desert, where all of the different animals come together for the common purpose of drinking water. If you are willing to get to know people better, use these locations to your advantage.

Common areas are great because, in general, you know when people will flock to them. Lunch, for example, is when most people use the microwaves to heat up their food. Why not drop by at the same time and strike up a conversation with someone who is waiting two to three minutes for a frozen burrito to warm up? The person isn't doing anything better anyway, so you won't be interrupting his or her work (if that's a concern of yours).

Another suggestion for taking opportunities to get to know people is to show up to formal events early. I know it may sound like a revolutionary idea, but you are totally allowed to come to church early if you want to. You could take this extra fifteen minutes to go mingle with people whom you'd never normally get a chance to speak to if you showed up right when the service starts. It's a super easy way to get to know more people, and all you have to do is leave your house fifteen minutes earlier than normal—anyone could do that!

It doesn't take much time to significantly increase the frequency and quality of our interactions with people. You don't have to set aside an additional two hours of your day to do this—just spend ten minutes more going to the people instead of making them come to you. A lot of people will *never* seek you out to connect with you—you have to go to them. That's just the way it is. If you want to help foster a connected environment in your organization, you're the one who's going to have to make it happen with some people.

If you're in any kind of leadership position in your organization, you don't have to wait for a handwritten invitation to connect with people—just go do it! Force yourself to go connect with others, even if it doesn't come naturally. Believe it or not, people actually would love to talk with you (unless you continually violate the principles in this book, but we are working on that, right?). Don't assume that you're "bothering" them. You're making yourself available. Now don't get me wrong, we can't be completely out of balance on this and spend more time chatting with people than working. It's been my experience, however, that many people in leadership positions are completely in the other ditch—they don't *ever* come by for casual conversation with the intent of getting to know you better.

THE POWER OF LUNCH

Everyone has to eat. Why not use this fact to your advantage to get to know the people around you better? In order to build out your Opportunity Tree, start inviting people to lunch on a regular basis and pay for it yourself. This accomplishes a couple of things. For starters, it communicates to them that they are important enough to you to eat lunch with. Second, because you are buying, it doesn't put any sort of burden on them—all they have to do is show up and get a free meal. I've found that people rarely say no to a free lunch.

How many times in the last year has someone offered to take *you* to a free lunch just to get to know you a little better? If you're like many of us, the answer is zero. Why is this? It could be because of money, but it also could be because it never crosses other people's minds to use lunch as an opportunity to connect with you. We shouldn't think we have to take someone to a four-star restaurant, either—a delicious burrito is just as effective if the intent is to simply spend more one-on-one time with a person. Remember the UIT? Well, by taking someone out to lunch, you are showing the individual that he is important enough to spend *both* your time and money on. Cha-ching!

Lunch is great because it's a solid thirty minutes to an hour of one-on-one communication, which we already know is the primary way to strengthen a relationship with someone. We literally can undo years of "weird" interactions with others just by going out to eat with them one time. Buying someone lunch is almost like some sort of magic cure-all. It instantly changes the dynamic of your relationship with that person, especially if the two of you have never gone to lunch before. Don't pass up this easy way to strengthen a connection with someone.

Lunch is a great opportunity for relaxed conversation. People don't feel as compelled to get back to their jobs while they are eating, so they are more open to talking about things that aren't related to work—just the kind of stuff that allows us to get to know them better! When we pluck them out of work and put them into a more casual environment, we might be surprised how much they open up about things in their lives—and this is mutually beneficial.

You have to use some wisdom here, of course (especially as a Christian). I personally *never* would take a woman out to lunch if it was just going to be the two of us. Since I'm married, it would be wrong for a couple of reasons. First, it just doesn't look right. Second, I wouldn't want my wife going out to eat with some guy, so I'm not going to do that to her. I've actually canceled lunch appointments before because a third person couldn't make it. Remember, people are great about filling in the blanks. If they see you in a compromising situation, some will make up a story, and it may not be a story you're comfortable with. I'm not trying to give you any hard and fast rules here; I'm just suggesting you use wisdom. If in doubt, take at least another person, preferably one who is the same gender as you.

The point of this entire chapter is that it is *our* responsibility to connect with the people around us, not theirs. Making our organizations the best place to work (or serve) is *not* just the responsibility of the people in positions of authority—it's everyone's responsibility. Leaders can create a framework and support the activities, but at the end of the day, everyone in the organization needs to be doing the things that will ensure everyone feels connected and valued. This doesn't happen by accident! It happens by doing all of the little things we know to do, day after day, in all of our interactions. Proactively connect with people—because if you're waiting for them to do it, it's most likely not going to happen.

18

Handling Conversation

I've noticed that some people feel uncomfortable engaging in even casual conversation with others. I don't think it's because they are bad communicators; I think it's because they don't feel like they have many options—things they *know* they can talk about in order to move a conversation along. None of us like to walk away from conversations thinking to ourselves, "What just happened?" Unfortunately, this happens too often to too many people. It happens to me less and less often now, but when it does, it's still a very uncomfortable feeling. It doesn't have to be this way, though. In this chapter, I'm going to give you some basic tools that you can use to put the odds in your favor when talking to other people. It's not going to be a comprehensive list, but it'll get you on your way to reducing those what-just-happened encounters.

SET THE TONE OF YOUR CONVERSATION

Just like you make a first impression with someone when you meet them for the first time, you also make a "first impression" with individuals each and every time you strike up a conversation with them. If you look angry, the person is going to prepare for an angry sort of conversation. If you look like you've been crying for the past thirty minutes, the person is going to prepare for a sad sort of conversation.

Now, if you approach a person with your head held high, a smile on your face, and a firm handshake, what sort of tone have you set for your conversation? A happy one!

Believe it or not, you communicate the tone of your conversation to another person before saying a single word. People are masters at reading body language and facial expressions—we've been doing it our whole lives. Be aware of what your nonverbals (or physical demeanor) are communicating to the person you are about to talk to.

When you are at church, think of how important it is to set a tone that reflects God's character when you talk to other believers and especially visitors. Don't be fake—just let the joy of God naturally come out of you. This is one of the key ways people are attracted to God. They see what God has done for you, and they say, "I want some of that!" Remembering your position in Christ will affect your overall disposition, which in turn will set the tone of your conversations with visitors appropriately. People like being around others who are happy.

If you're a born-again Christian, you should not spend any significant period of time being sad or discouraged. Why? Because whatever problems Christians experience in this life are fleeting. God, speaking through James, said of our lives (in James 4:14, NKJV): "whereas you do not know what will happen tomorrow. For what is your life? It is even a vapor that appears for a little time and then vanishes away." From an eternal standpoint, our lives on the earth wouldn't even show up as a tiny blip on a radar. God does want us to be healthy, happy, and productive in this life, but even if we aren't experiencing everything God wants us to now, we still can look forward to an eternity with Him in heaven. How wonderful is that! This life is temporary; any problems you are experiencing now will be over soon regardless of how big they may seem. Focus on the positive, and your interactions are more likely to start off on the right foot. You can choose to be happy regardless of what's going on around you.

GET THE FOCUS OFF OF YOU

Remember in previous chapters where we talked about how most people are primarily only concerned about their own wants and needs?

They like to talk about what they're interested in more than anything or anyone else. Well, this goes for us, too! If we don't watch out, we could turn a conversation that was intended to form a relationship with someone else into a personal therapy session where we unload all of our problems on an unsuspecting victim. This is a *major* turnoff to people, and it doesn't do anything to get us closer to our goal of making them feel like they are important. When getting to know people, we have to be willing to not be at the center of the conversation.

People *really* like to be listened to. They like it when people pay attention to them, and they literally will talk for hours about what they're interested in. Let them do that, if that's what they want to do initially. Remember, it's all about them at this point. They won't talk forever; but even if they did, that's OK—they most likely will walk away from the conversation with a good impression of you because you listened to them the whole time.

For some people, listening is *very* difficult because they've spent their entire lives trying to talk about themselves as much as possible—they have to change after decades of self-focused behavior. From a practical standpoint, if we are trying to learn more about another person, any time we spend talking about ourselves is not moving us closer to that objective. In order to connect with people, we need to do a lot of listening. How can we understand others if we don't give them the opportunity to express themselves?

I think people may feel the need to constantly "sell" themselves to others because they believe that's how they're going to get people interested in them. In reality, others often become defensive or competitive. If our goal is to connect with people, we need to listen to them—really listen, not "listen" like someone who's just waiting for his or her turn to talk. The next chapter is dedicated to the topic of listening, and I'll give you some great examples of how to demonstrate to people that you are actively listening to them.

A lot of freedom can be gained by realizing that people become more interested in us when we listen to them rather than when we constantly dominate our conversations by talking about ourselves. When we become interested in other people, they suddenly become interested in us. Humans are always on the lookout for individuals they can connect with. When we find those people, we want to keep them close because they make us feel more affirmed as individuals. When others are interested in us when we speak, the next step is to make them our friends—and everyone likes to have more friends. If we don't show an interest in the conversation phase, we'll never become friends.

ASK QUESTIONS

One of the key ways to get to know more about people is to ask questions (surprise, surprise). In general, people like answering questions about themselves, and asking questions shows that we are interested in them—a double score! We don't even have to make up the questions on the spot, either—at least not the first round of them.

Have a game plan *before* you are in a situation where you'll be engaging in a bunch of conversations. If you are the type of person who has trouble talking to people, this takes a ton of pressure off of you because you've already decided on a half dozen questions you could use to get conversations going. Put the odds in your favor! You don't have to avoid people—you can just approach them and ask the questions you've already prepared.

For instance, I have learned that parents really like to talk about their kids. When I talk with people, one of the first questions I'll ask is whether they have any kids. If they do, it gets real easy from there on out because I just start asking questions about their kids. Dads will beam about how great their daughters are at soccer. Moms will go on and on about whatever phase their kids are in and all of the challenges the women face trying to deal with them. You can almost put the conversation on autopilot once you get parents talking about their kids.

If you're at church, two common questions people ask are: "Hello, I don't believe we've met before—what's your name?" and "How long have you been coming here?"

For some of you, this seems like common sense, but you might be surprised how many people actively avoid others because they feel uncomfortable talking to people. In the cases where they do approach others, the conversations can be awkward, and they may leave feeling embarrassed at what just took place. Do not assume that all people are slick conversationalists, because they are not.

Another great technique you could use if you know you'll be talking to a specific person is to find out things about him or her before you meet. When you do meet, you could ask about those things. It's simple to do, and it can leave a good taste in the mouth of the individual. For instance, if you will be meeting with a prospective business client, and you find out the person likes to ski, you could ask a question like: "I heard you like to ski. What is your favorite place to go skiing?" Things like this earn you influence with the individual—influence that may ultimately land you the deal. Don't leave interactions up to chance; put them in your favor as much as possible.

Look at it like you're jump-starting the process of getting to know others. I know it may seem a bit contrived, but most initial conversation is small talk anyway—it's not like you'll be offending anyone with standard questions. People have come to expect certain questions when they first meet someone, so much so that you'd make an odd impression on them if you tried asking them something out of the ordinary. Just stick with what works for the first couple of rounds.

After a couple of rounds of small talk, you usually will hear something you can use as a springboard into a more specific topic. For instance, if you ask a woman how her day is going, and she then says a plane flew into her house this morning, you now have the opportunity to start asking more questions about the information she just divulged. (For example: "A plane? Did anyone get hurt?") See? Not hard at all.

I've had some people ask me, "What if other people just keep asking you questions and always deflect questions about themselves?" Well, we definitely don't want to start a communication arms race where each side avoids answering questions. My advice, in this case, is to answer their questions and try to slip in a few of your own to make the conversation as balanced as possible. Good old common sense will serve you well here. If a person refuses to answer any question at all, you don't want to make it any weirder than it may already be—just answer the questions honestly and recognize that the other person may be trying out some of the same principles you have just learned.

19

How to Be a Better Listener

> *Conversation in the United States is a competitive exercise in which the first person to draw breath is declared the listener.*
> —Nathan Miller

America is a nation of poor listeners. Whether we choose not to listen, or if we never learned how to properly listen in the first place, it's creating barriers between us and the people we attempt to communicate with. In this chapter, I'm going to give you some listening techniques you can use to demonstrate that you're paying attention to what others are saying. This is important because when people feel like they are heard and understood, they feel more connected and less frustrated. You'll be able to use all of these techniques today!

The only job of a listener is to be physically, mentally, and spiritually present when someone is talking. There is a better way to listen, just as there is a better way to speak. We are not born good listeners; we have to learn how to be. Many of us learned poor listening behaviors from poor listeners, and that's all we know—no one ever showed us a better way.

We are told (in James 1:19, NKJV), "So then, my beloved brethren, let every man be swift to hear, slow to speak, slow to wrath." James outlined some of the characteristics needed to be successful in life. There are multiple pieces of wisdom in this Scripture, but we're going to focus on the first piece: Be swift to hear. Sometimes it's worth reminding ourselves that Scripture is inspired by God. He wanted us to know that being quick to listen to Him, and others inspired by Him, is an important component in experiencing God's life in our lives more abundantly. That Scripture isn't in the Bible because God needed to pad out the book to make it larger—it's there to help us. If we are bad listeners, it's in our own best interest to fix that because we'll be well on our way to better and more productive lives.

Becoming a better listener isn't only limited to hearing things inspired by God. Becoming a better listener is one of the foundational components of being a better communicator in general. We still have to use wisdom when choosing *what* to listen to, but if we've already decided we want to listen to someone (a spouse, co-worker, etc.), we may as well do it to the best of our ability. According to James, we should put a higher priority on listening than on speaking.

One of my all-time favorite proverbs is Proverbs 17:28 (NKJV), "Even a fool is counted wise when he holds his peace; when he shuts his lips, he is considered perceptive." Do you want people to consider you wise? Well, one of the easiest ways to achieve that is to talk less and listen more. If you aren't speaking, no one can judge what you say. You can't stop talking altogether, but you can choose when you speak and for how long. People will perceive you as wise the more you listen and the less you speak.

The more we talk, the more likely we could say something that could cause us problems—it's just a percentages game. "In the multitude of words sin is not lacking, but he who restrains his lips is wise" (Proverbs 10:19, NKJV). The more we talk, the more problems we could cause ourselves. Being good listeners is not only good from a relational standpoint but also keeps us from saying things we might regret later.

ARE YOU REALLY LISTENING?

When people talk to you, do you really listen to them? Or, are you just waiting to speak? Think about that for a minute. When someone is talking, are you actively participating in the conversation? Or, are you (1) thinking about a point you wanted to make awhile ago, (2) trying to figure out when you can squeeze in what you want to say, or (3) not listening at all (you are thinking about something completely different but nodding like you're paying attention)? (Personally speaking, I usually was in group number 3 above.)

If we ever hope to connect with people on a deeper level and positively influence them to a greater degree, we must understand them better. In order to understand them better, we need to listen to them more. If we aren't hearing people with the intent of understanding them, how can we expect to connect with them on more than a superficial level?

People seem to know when they've been heard and understood. We can innately sense when others have been actively listening to us, internalized what we've said, and given us the appropriate signals (verbal and nonverbal) that indicate they've heard and understood us. How many times have you talked to a person and walked away saying to yourself, "He didn't hear a word I said." Oh, he heard all right; he just didn't listen. This kind of hearing creates barriers in organizations. If you do this long enough, people will become frustrated and find ways to work around you. Listening to others is a key component to increasing your influence with them.

LISTEN WITH YOUR BODY

The first technique we'll cover has to do with the messages you send to another person with your body. There are physical queues we can give to others to demonstrate we're actively listening to them. If we don't do them, people will notice their absence and leave the conversation feeling like we might not have understood what they were trying to communicate.

In the 1960s, Dr. Albert Mehrabian of UCLA conducted a study to determine how much of our communications of feelings and attitudes are based on nonverbals (tone of voice, facial expressions, etc.). He determined that 93 percent of those communications are nonverbal and only 7 percent are verbal. There are some disagreements regarding how applicable these numbers are to *all* of our communications, but when we consider how often our feelings and attitudes are a part of our daily conversations, it's easy to see how important nonverbal signals are to successfully communicate with another person. If you were to say the words "I'm fine" through clenched teeth while glaring at the person who asked you, what would come across to the listener is that you actually were not fine. This same concept is true with regards to listening.

Picture this: You're talking to your husband, and he is saying things like, "Yes, uh-huh, keep going," but he is looking all over the place the entire time trying to find someone. Is he really listening to you? No! His actions are not in alignment with his words. To be effective communicators, we don't want to send mixed messages to the people we are listening to. Demonstrate to them that you are listening. Now, let's talk about some specific ways we can do that.

I hope this is obvious, but if you can't hear the other person due to the environment you're in, move to a different location. Just say something like: "I'm having a tough time hearing you. Can we move to the break room?" This is important because without the right environment, you're not going to hear the message correctly—which is the main reason for communicating in the first place. It also conveys to others that what they have to say to you is important, and you want to hear it. Don't try to yell at each other over some pre-service music if you can avoid it.

When people talk to you, face them. This demonstrates that they have your attention. Squarely face the other person with your feet and shoulders. If you point your feet away from the person, this conveys that you want to leave, because your feet typically point to where you want to go. If you squarely face people, you are actively engaging them with your body. You're saying, "I am here, and I am listening to you."

We see this concept play out in groups of people. When many people are talking together, they naturally form a circle with all of the people in it. If you are part of the circle, you are part of the conversation. If you are outside of the circle, you are not part of the conversation. Squarely facing a person with your feet and shoulders is like creating a small, two-person communication circle.

Look people in the eyes when you are talking with them. This is one of the most important nonverbals you can give to a speaker.

Doing this sends the message that you are actively engaged, and they have your undivided attention. Looking all over the place or doing something else while they are talking to you communicates to them that they aren't that important to you—or at least whatever they are talking about at the moment isn't that important.

If there is too much going on to look at people when you're talking with them, such as at the end of a church service, tell them you're having a hard time focusing because of all the commotion—they'll understand. You could tell them you are interested in what they have to say, but you'll have to change venues. You could invite them to coffee or lunch. Heck, you could ask them for their e-mail address or phone number to follow up with them later. This at least demonstrates to them that you *do* care about what they are trying to say, while acknowledging the environment is inhibiting the communication. Pretending you're paying attention when you're not isn't good for either of you. Odds are they'll notice.

Another nonverbal that's easy to address is crossing our arms. In short, don't do it—it can be perceived as being standoffish and protective. In Joe Navarro's book *What Every Body is Saying*, he said that leaving your arms relaxed at your sides is an effective way of communicating to speakers that you are no threat to them—it helps put them at ease. This is especially important when approaching someone for the first time. We want to do everything in our power to make the person feel comfortable.

In general, avoid doing anything that could send a wrong message to the person you're supposed to be listening to. Don't adjust your clothes (unless something is embarrassingly wrong), don't play on your smartphone, and don't comb your hair or do other sorts of preening activities (trimming your nails, picking at your hands, etc.).

The last tip for listening with your body has to do with listening while seated. If you are talking with someone while you're sitting, it is good practice to sit up straight and lean forward a little with both feet on the ground. Leaning forward shows the person you're physically anticipating what is going to be said—you're interested! Act like the person is about ready to give you the winning lottery numbers—your posture would be that of anticipation and excitement. If you have a notepad with you, it may be appropriate to put it in front of you and have your writing instrument available to take notes, if necessary. People *really* like it when you take notes when they speak. It physically communicates that what they are saying is so important you want to make sure to write down anything you might forget later.

Do not slouch in your chair. (Think of the stereotypical, rebellious teenager!) This sends a loud and clear: "This discussion is boring me. Can I leave now?" You might be surprised how many full-grown adults I see doing this on a regular basis. It's easy to fix, so there is no reason not to. Remember the Golden Rule. If you don't like it when people slouch when you're talking to them, don't do it to others. Who likes talking to an audience full of people who are communicating to you through nonverbals that they don't want to be there? Not me!

DON'T INTERRUPT

My family will tell you that interrupting me while I'm talking is a surefire way to get under my skin. The more I became aware of many of the better-listening tips we're talking about, the more I noticed poor habits happening all around me—and the faster I became annoyed with them. My family and I are trying to be better listeners, but each of us have years of bad listening habits under our belts, and it's going to take some time to relearn how to listen properly.

Interrupting people while they are talking, usually so you can say what you want to say, is just flat-out rude. I still do it sometimes, but I'm better than I used to be. How are people supposed to interpret being cut off before they can finish what they wanted to say? Not only do they dislike it, but you're demonstrating to them that what they are currently talking about isn't very important to you because you've decided to stop them right in their tracks and say something of your own. What you are saying, in not so many words, is "Yeah, yeah, whatever you're saying is fine, but let *me* tell you something more important."

Interrupting people creates another arms race. Now people understand that if they want to finish what they were talking about, they either have to talk faster or interrupt you to finish saying what they started to say before you interrupted them. Perhaps what the person was saying was inspired by God, and you just missed a major breakthrough in your life because you couldn't wait the extra minute to hear the rest.

Instead of interrupting, be patient. I know sometimes it may seem like you just "have to" interject something into a conversation at that very moment, but in reality, you typically don't. If you have some scratch paper or a notebook, write down your points; you can come back around when that person is done and share your thoughts then. Let the person who is talking finish—you'll get your chance to speak.

Some people have expressed concern that, when talking with certain individuals, they may *never* get a chance to speak if they don't interrupt. I know these types of people, too. It's very rare, though, that I *never* get a chance to talk—it's just that I have to wait longer to do it. If you happen to be leading a group discussion, it may be helpful to remind the participants up front that everybody's input is welcome. In the end, however, if someone completely dominates a conversation, and you have important information to share, you may have to continue the conversation later or through a different channel. Maybe you will need to send an e-mail or text. The last thing we want to do, however, is constantly cut people off, because that sends the wrong message: You aren't important enough to listen to.

If you are constantly on the receiving end of being cut off, I feel for you. I really do. With certain people I talk with, it seems like I'm being interrupted on *every single statement*. Do you know how frustrating that is? Instead of effectively communicating, what I want to do is run out the front door screaming, so I can let out all of the built-up frustration. In order to maturely deal with it, I try to find a "happy place." What I attempt to do is realize the person just communicates that way right now. I need to accept that I'll probably be interrupted continually during our conversation, so I need to prepare for it. Sometimes that little mental adjustment can be enough to get me through it.

Lastly, we might want to check how long we talk when we're engaged in conversations. We most definitely do *not* want to talk for so long that other people never get a chance to speak and feel like their only option is to interrupt us. If you think you're talking too much, you probably are.

GIVE VOCAL QUEUES

The next tip is something many of us do to a certain degree naturally: Give small "queues" when listening to others to let them know we are following what they're saying. Instead of doing it unintentionally, we now will be able to do it more consciously and deliberately.

When talking with someone, it's appropriate to say things like "Yes," "I see," and "What happened next?" at appropriate intervals. We do this to show others that we are mentally engaged in what they are saying and that we understand what has just been said. People expect these sorts of queues, too. I know some people who don't say a single thing when I talk to them, and it's just flat-out weird. I sometimes wonder if they have fallen asleep with their eyes open. It's actually distracting to talk to someone like that, but I just roll with it to the best of my ability.

At all times during our conversations, we want to communicate to the speaker that we are present and listening. Periodic feedback is necessary to keep the conversation rolling. When those who are speaking hear our "I see," they interpret that as an "I understand what you're saying," and they feel comfortable moving on to the next thing they want to say. Without these little queues, they are left wondering if you understand what has been said or if you even heard it at all. Don't do that to the person you're listening to.

DEMONSTRATE YOU UNDERSTAND

In addition to offering small vocal queues to give a speaker feedback, you can use another technique to demonstrate to a speaker that you are fully engaged in what he or she is saying. It's not difficult, but it will take a conscious effort on your part initially to make sure you are doing it. Like most things, you're going to have to make yourself do it until it becomes a habit.

One of the most surefire ways to demonstrate to a speaker that you understand is to quickly paraphrase what has been said at different points in the conversation. This serves two purposes: (1) It allows you to prove that you've been paying attention; and (2) If your understanding is incorrect, it gives the other person a chance to correct you. In a way, it's similar to using the steering wheel to keep your car on a straight road. The little tiny corrections keep you from ending up in a ditch. If you periodically paraphrase what has been said, it keeps you from getting too far away from the intent of the speaker—you "correct" your understanding (or at least check to make sure you're still on course).

As an example, let's say your employer approaches you about the work you've done on a recent graphic design project. He is concerned because the project you just printed isn't what he had in mind for the promotion, and he doesn't believe it is in line with the company's branding identity. After awhile, you paraphrase what he has said by saying something like: "So, you don't think this reflects our company's brand because of the choice of colors I used. You'd also like me to put more emphasis on (a specific aspect of) the promotion and show you the changes on Thursday." The person then will either agree with you or correct your understanding by restating what he is trying to communicate. See how this works? It's like you're taking the temperature of the speaker at various times to make sure both of you are talking about the same thing. Sometimes *what* someone is trying to say and *how* he is saying it are way off, and paraphrasing back to him what you *think* he has said can do wonders for making sure his intent is coming across correctly.

When I first learned about this technique in Robert Bolton's book *People Skills: How to Assert Yourself, Listen to Others, and Resolve Conflicts*, I was a little apprehensive concerning its effectiveness. To me, it seemed sort of odd to blurt out a statement telling someone basically what he already had said (though in a much-condensed form). Well, I was wrong. The people I've talked with haven't thought anything of it. In fact, they seemed to appreciate the feedback because it meant someone actually listened to them for a change. Give it a try for yourself. Like anything else, it may take a little bit of practice to figure out the appropriate places to paraphrase—but when you do, you'll show the people you are talking with that you understand them.

DON'T HIJACK THE CONVERSATION

When someone hijacks an airplane, what happens? Well, a person on board a plane forcibly takes control of the aircraft and announces that everyone is going to a different destination. The exact same thing happens all the time when people are talking. One person will be talking about something, and another person will change the topic to talk about what he wants instead. This is called hijacking the conversation. It's another poor-listening habit we are going to try to break.

Hijacking conversations is so prevalent that I'm not sure most people even recognize it's happening anymore. People are so used to starting to talk about something and then having a listener change subjects on them that they often don't even stop to say, "Hey, I wanted to keep talking about X, Y, and Z." What happens instead is they have to attempt to hijack the conversation back to what they originally were talking about. This creates a conversational mess because we never stay on a subject long enough to let each person finish. The whole point of the interaction is missed because both parties are focused on talking and neither is listening, so it seems like you're bouncing all over the place.

Constantly hijacking conversations to talk about what we want to talk about is pure selfishness. We already covered why selfishness is bad in chapter 8. Let's stay as far away from selfishness as possible! Let's put—and keep—the focus on the other person as a sign of respect and love. Let people finish what they are saying. We'll get our chance to comment. After one subject is finished, a new one naturally will evolve—just make sure to give others all of the time they need to finish the train of thoughts in their heads. People really will appreciate this.

I understand that conversation is fluid and you can't put hard and fast limits on what takes place during the course of one. We can fix a lot of common problems, though, by walking into a conversation with the intent of listening more and by not violating the handful of principles I just gave you. One of the primary ways we learn is by listening. If we can see the value in and be willing to learn more about the people around us to connect with them on more than a superficial level, we need to be actively engaged listeners.

20

A Happy Countenance

What is your "countenance"? The *Merriam-Webster Dictionary* defines it as this:

> **countenance:** *the appearance of a person's face: a person's expression*

Your countenance is the expression you wear on your face. In face-to-face communication, before a word is even said to another individual, your countenance arrives first and gives the person some clues as to what type of person you are and what type of mood you are in. It's another one of those nonverbal-communication factors we talked about in the last chapters. If you're not paying attention to the expression on your face, you might be creating barriers to your communication before you even say your first word.

All things being equal, people would rather be around others who are happy. Does anyone really like being around people who constantly are preaching doom and gloom and look like the last place they want to be is the place they currently are? No! Happiness and a positive outlook are contagious. The happier you are, the more ability you have to positively affect the people around you.

You might be thinking, "But Tony, I'm not very happy, because things aren't going that well for me." I understand, but carrying that around on your face is not helping you or anyone around you. In reality, it's probably making things worse. Remember in chapter 4, we talked about the thought life and how it determines our reality? What are you thinking about all day? Are you thinking about how you're a born-again Christian with power in *this life* to change your circumstances for the better? Are you thinking about how any problem you're currently facing is temporary, and in a thousand years (oftentimes even a month from now), you're not even going to care about what's troubling you now? Or, are you continually focusing on everything that is not going right in your life? The quickest way to become unhappy is to allow yourself to think about things that make you unhappy (surprise!). Focus on happy things, and you get happier. Focus on sad things, and you get sadder.

I'm not trying to trivialize situations like the passing of loved ones and other traumatic events. There is a natural mourning and healing period associated with some experiences, so I'm not trying to tell you to just "get over it" as soon as they happen. As Christians, we are told that God will never leave us nor forsake us (Deuteronomy 31:6), and that He walks with us through hard times (Psalms 23:4). We are never alone in any situation, which can be comforting when our happiness seems to be getting siphoned away by the trials of life. Most causes of unhappy expressions are far less deep than someone passing, though. They usually are caused by kid (or other relationship) troubles, money troubles, health troubles, or selfishness. These things can be addressed with tweaks to how we think.

SMILE

One of the easiest things you can do to spread some of your cheer is to smile. That's right, just a big ol' smile can do wonders for the people you come in contact with all day long.

Smiling communicates to others around you that you aren't a threat and that you have good intentions. Yes, I realize that some people use this fact to manipulate others, but that shouldn't be our motive as Christians. Our smiles can be genuine and communicate our intentions of goodwill. We are God's ambassadors on the earth—why wouldn't we be happy?

As I previously stated in chapter 18, a smile puts the tone of any conversation immediately in your favor. You walk into a conversation with a big smile on your face, and people *expect* to have a good exchange with you—you set the stage for the interaction. If your goal is to be better with people, why not use every tool at your disposal? If you want your interactions with others to improve, this is what it looks like in your day-to-day life. This is a concrete example of how to be more skillful with people—smile more!

The more you smile, the more you will notice that people will smile back at you—it's almost an automatic response. Try it the next time you are walking down the hall at church or work. Make eye contact with someone who isn't smiling, say "Good morning," and smile at him. What will happen? That's right, he will smile back at you! Sure, for some people it will be a fake, forced response, but you still can affect them with *your* smile.

For people who have been dealing with junk all day long, you can be like a beacon of light in a dark room. People are drawn to others who are happy. I think it's because they want some of that happiness to rub off on them, and it can! Personally speaking, when I'm around someone who is happy, I leave the conversation feeling like my internal battery has been charged a little. We can do that for other people. If you really are happy and just don't show it, then this is a quick fix for you. Start wearing your happiness on the outside and use it to positively influence the people around you.

WHAT DO YOU THINK ABOUT ALL DAY?

It's really hard when you think about sad and depressing things all day long to then try to force yourself to be happy. We've already covered the importance of controlling our thoughts because if we think about the wrong stuff, the next step is to act on those wrong thoughts, and we don't want to do that. If you're sad on the inside and tired of faking it on the outside, maybe you need to analyze what you think about all day long.

A Christian teacher once made the comment that the mind is like a set of binoculars, and anything you "point" yours at will become the biggest thing to you. There is a lot of wisdom in this saying. It acknowledges that *we* have control over where we point our binoculars (minds). That's right, we don't have to watch two hours of overly negative news every night. We don't have to focus on how our co-workers are grating on our nerves. We can choose what we look at. If we focus on the negative, the negative will get bigger. If we focus on the positive, the positive will get bigger.

We can see this play out again and again in life. Have you ever met someone who was dissatisfied with his pay at a job? His dissatisfaction started out as a simple thought. However, if he were to choose to focus on that thought, it would grow bigger in his mind. Eventually, the dissatisfaction may become so big that he feels like he "has to" do something about it, and he may end up leaving to go somewhere else because of it. Sometimes people will leave for worse jobs that may pay a little more but are a demotion overall! How does this happen? By constantly thinking about their dissatisfaction, they make it bigger and bigger until it is a major problem (for them, anyway) that has to be dealt with.

I'm not saying you should stay at a job that's taking advantage of you. First and foremost, be led by God. Express your desire for a better-paying job and then wait for Him to tell you what to do. A major tactic of the enemy is to try to make you feel like you're backed into a corner where you have to make a decision this very second. In reality, you have all the time in the world to be led by God. Hasty emotional decisions are a recipe for disaster.

In John 8:1–11, we read about how Jesus found Himself in the middle of a trap set for Him by the religious leaders of the day. The Pharisees brought to Him a woman caught in the act of adultery and asked Jesus what they should do with her. They thought they had Him trapped because the standard punishment dictated by the law of Moses was that she (and the adulterer) should be stoned to death. They assumed Jesus either had to say, "Stone her" or "Let her go," because in their minds, there were no other choices. Both were bad options for Jesus. He couldn't tell them to ignore the law, and He couldn't condemn her to death, because His ministry was completely based on truth, compassion, and grace.

Picture the scenario in your head. Jesus was in the temple at the time when a group of men dragged a woman in there—it must have been quite the spectacle! I highly doubt they politely asked Jesus what should be done, either. I suspect they were hammering Him with questions like: "What do we do? Answer us! Quick, tell us what to do! Do we kill her or let her go? What do we do? What do we do!" Do you know what Jesus did? He bent down and wrote on the ground with His finger. I have no proof, but I'm guessing He was asking God what to do.

Jesus stood up and gave the only answer that could have saved the woman and the integrity of His ministry: "He who is without sin among you, let him throw a stone at her first" (John 8:7, NKJV). This wasn't even one of the choices! That's God for you. The Pharisees ended up leaving one by one because no one was willing to become a public hypocrite. An angry mob was completely dismantled by a few words from God.

The enemy does this exact same thing to people all day long. He presents us with two (or more) bad options and then tries to get us to pick one of them because "you have no other choice." Says who—the one who's trying to destroy your life? When you feel trapped in your thought life by only seemingly bad choices, don't choose any of them! Instead, look to God for guidance and ask Him for your "he-who-is-without-sin" solution, just as Jesus did.

Always check yourself to make sure you are not spending too much time focused on one negative aspect of your job while disregarding all of the other great things in your current position. Maybe you work with great people. Maybe you have a flexible schedule. Maybe work is only five minutes away from your house. Try focusing on those things a little more and bring some balance to the equation. Don't get trapped into thinking that your situation is so bad you have to make a decision right now—you don't!

We can choose what we focus on in many other areas of our lives, too. If you are married, do you tend to focus almost exclusively on the things about your spouse that bother you? What would happen if you started focusing on the things that don't bother you? Your entire disposition toward your spouse would start to change because you'd shrink the negatives and grow the positives. Instead of constantly focusing on how your husband leaves dirty dishes on the table or makes a mess in the bathroom, why don't you focus on things such as how he's a dedicated family man who makes a good living for your family, and how he loves you and the kids? It may seem silly to even point that out, but some people seriously struggle with situations exactly like this. They may have amazing spouses, yet they spend all of their time focusing on their spouses' weaknesses instead of their strengths. That's a recipe for dissatisfaction.

One of the best things I ever did to positively affect my overall mood was to stop watching the news. As I mentioned in chapter 3, I'd sit in front of the TV for one to two hours a night and listen to all of the terrible things happening in the world. It was affecting my outlook on life in a very negative way. I'm so much happier now that I'm not pouring hours of garbage into my brain every night. With the state of technology nowadays, there is no reason why we have to let someone else pick what kind of news we should watch—we can subscribe to the subjects we are interested in. My new smartphone came with a news app that lets me pick which topics I'm interested in. The same thing can be done on a computer. I'm not trying to hide from the real world. Bad things have been happening since long before I was born. Do I really have to hear about every single one of them every night? No.

Do you want to change how happy you are right now? If you're a born-again Christian, why don't you say this out loud a few times: "God, thank you for loving *me*. Your Word says you will never leave me nor forsake me. Thank you for having a purpose for my life. I thank you that you hear me every time I pray. Thank you for saving me and securing my eternity with you in heaven. You are a good God, and you have good plans for me. I am no accident. With you, I am an overcomer—the first, not the last. Everything I put my hand to is blessed." How do you feel now? If that doesn't work for you, go read Psalm 91 a few times and tell me if you aren't a little happier when you're done. Do you see how changing what you think about affects your attitude? If you want to be happier, think about the happier things in your life.

Lastly, the prophet Isaiah said (in Isaiah 26:3, NKJV), "You will keep him in perfect peace, whose mind is stayed on You, because he trusts in You." Do you want more peace in your life? Well, according to this Scripture, the best way to experience peace is to stay your mind on God. Is there a part of you that worries all day long while you are at work? Well, use that part to think about the goodness of God and His Word, instead. Learn a few Scriptures that really resonate with you and repeat those to yourself throughout the day, instead of focusing on what's not going right in your life. If you continually focus on God throughout the day, you'll notice your attitude will naturally change to align with His Word. As you find Scriptures to repeat to yourself, you may also find that God already has given you instruction on how to deal with your problem. Read more of God's Word and let that bounce around in your head all day long—it'll change you from the inside out.

21

The Power of Names

What we'll talk about in this chapter has been one of the most fruitful concepts for me personally. Who would have thought you could make such a huge impact on others just by doing simple things like remembering their names? It sounds trivial, but its effect is quite profound. You can turn a cold work environment into a warm, lively atmosphere by doing nothing more than remembering names and using them whenever you see people.

Remembering people's names instantly separates you from others. Instead of being one of the dozens of people others casually pass by each day, you become someone who *knows* them. Sure, you don't know them on a deep level, but learning their names is the first step in that process. At some point, *every* person in your life was a stranger. You first had to find out each of their names and then use their names to communicate with them on a personal level.

Names immediately break down barriers with people you don't talk with very often. When you know someone's name and use it, you create a warm atmosphere in which you can learn a little more about the person. There is no reason you have to keep seeing the same people day after day without learning their names. It makes it less weird for everyone involved. You know what's more uncomfortable than asking someone his name? Seeing someone ten times a day in the break room and not knowing who he is!

You might be surprised how many people will completely ignore you—won't talk to you or look you in the eyes—until you learn their names. Learning someone's name is the price of admission to a more fulfilling relationship with him or her. People literally will spend years not talking to people they work around just because they don't know their names. Be the initiator—learn people's names and make your environment a little less weird for everyone.

JUST ASK

Do you realize I have never had someone refuse to give me his name when I asked? That's right, zero times. Even complete strangers I've never seen before have no problem giving me their names. I don't have some special power over people, either—I just ask.

Stop avoiding people and come right out and ask them their names—it saves you a bunch of awkward conversations in the future. One of my personal favorite approaches is this: "I see you around here all the time, and I realized I have never asked you your name. What's your name?" That's it. Nothing fancy, super witty, or funny—I just ask. Every single time, they give me their names. If you're worried about someone rejecting you, don't be.

I constantly hear people say things like: "I've been working here a year and see that guy every day, and I don't know his name. We even talk all the time." This is easy to fix. Just ask him his name.

Proactively asking people their names can save us from embarrassment later on, when we may find ourselves in a situation where the other person realizes we don't know his name and we should. Situations like this can occur when you least expect it, such as when you are introducing people and you can't identify the person you've been talking to for a year. This can be very uncomfortable for you, and it also demonstrates to the person (whose name you didn't bother to learn) that he wasn't important enough to you to learn who he is.

DEMONSTRATE PEOPLE ARE IMPORTANT TO YOU

If someone has told you his name, and you forgot it, he'll probably give you a break the next time you see him. However, if you continue to forget his name, the message you're sending to the other person is clear: "You're not important enough to me to remember your name." Ouch. When we *choose* to forget someone's name, we *choose* to send the message that the person isn't important to us.

When I first started working at my current company, I remember one day I was walking by the main door to our floor and saw our CEO coming on his little scooter (he had hurt his leg). Like a good corporate citizen, I rushed to open the door for him, so he wouldn't have to figure out how to do that while getting his scooter through at the same time. When I opened the door, he said something to me that forever changed my opinion of him as a person. He said, "Thank you, Tony." I didn't know whether to cry or hug him. He knew my name! He knew who I was! Never, ever underestimate the power of someone's name, especially if you are in a position of authority in your organization.

Remembering people's names demonstrates they're important to you. A name, in a very general way, represents a person as a whole. When you use people's names, you address them as individuals and show them they're not just expendable employees or volunteers.

NAMES PERSONALIZE INTERACTIONS

Names are so important to people that we should *find* ways to incorporate them into our everyday interactions. Whenever possible, in any sort of interaction with another individual, try to squeeze in his or her name. You may think this would cause your interactions to seem unnatural, but actually it doesn't. You can easily personalize each and every one of your interactions using simple techniques like these.

When you pass by someone at work, use her name. Instead of ignoring her or just giving her a "Hey," say something like, "What's up, Kate?" See the difference? You actually are accomplishing three things with a statement like this: (1) You're showing her that you remember her name, which may not be a big deal for people you've known a long time, but it is important to people you rarely talk to; (2) Said with a smile, it's a nice way to brighten up someone's day; and (3) It personalizes the interaction.

Whenever possible, use names. Don't be all weird about it and try to say the name an unnatural amount of times, but do be thinking about how you could use it more often. It's typically very easy to either start or finish an interaction with a name, so don't miss those opportunities.

If you meet with Susan to discuss a project, finish the conversation with something like, "Thanks for helping, Susan." Rather than just saying, "Thanks," you have now personalized the conversation by using her name.

These kinds of suggestions might seem sort of trivial to some people, but things like this are what separate those who are good with people from those who are not. If we develop good habits in all of our smaller interactions, the bigger ones will be much easier to navigate because we already have gained a small amount of influence with the people around us. Don't think that becoming more skillful with people is just about successfully handling the big interactions (such as consoling a person when a loved one passes away)—it's not. It's about consistently doing all of the little things we know to do each and every day, whether we feel like it or not.

THE 'MILLION-DOLLAR TEST'

Let's say you and I were in a room, and I announced that I had a little test for you. I sat you down in a chair and brought in ten other people you had never met before and lined them up in front of you. I then said: "Here's the game: Each one of these people will take turns saying his or her name one time. Tomorrow, we'll all come back into this room, and if you can give me their names, I'll give you one million dollars. You can use whatever you want to help you remember their names." Do you think you could do it? Of course you could! Why? Because now it's important to you. You might use your smartphone, write the names down on paper, or etch them on the wall with a piece of metal—anything you could think of!

It's not that we can't remember names. It's that we don't want to because we don't see the value in it. We never learned that remembering people's names is one of the easiest ways to gain positive influence with others, and it costs us nothing.

Right now, I'm sure some people are thinking, "But Tony, I meet too many people at one time to remember all of their names." I understand and have been there myself—especially after a church service. If you're being overwhelmed by too many new people at once, the strategy I like to use is this: Just learn one name. That's right, instead of taking a complete loss on all of your interactions, just remember one person's name. Write it down or put it in your phone. Just do your best to remember a single name.

TIPS FOR REMEMBERING MORE NAMES

One way I've found that helps me to remember people's names is to identify when I'm in a situation where I need to remember names and then put myself into a different mindset. For example, when I'm buying something at a restaurant, I think to myself, "I'm going to pay attention when the waitress introduces herself to us, and it's very important that I remember her name." I put myself into a sort of "name-remembering zone." I make it a big deal and, as a result, I'm now much better at remembering names than I used to be.

There is a restaurant my family and I frequent where we have used this very tactic with great results. Every time we show up, it's like the place turns into a party! People start talking to us, asking how things are going. The manager will ask about things we talked about during our last visit. Waitresses will even stop by our table just to talk. I feel like we get the "A+ treatment" for no other reason than we just learned their names. There is absolutely nothing special about what we did—we just asked the employees their names and then remembered them. That's it!

Another good approach I have used is to keep a list of people's names at my desk. Whenever I meet someone new at work and think I may have trouble remembering his or her name, I immediately write it down when I come back to my desk. Periodically, I'll review the list to make sure I haven't forgotten any names. It's simple to do, and I find I need my list far less than I first thought I would.

When you meet someone for the first time and he tells you his name, try to associate the name with something or someone else with the same name. Our brains are really good at this. When you see the person the next time, instead of trying to recall his name, your brain will bring the association back to you, and his name will be attached to that association. For example, if someone tells me his name is Luke, I'll associate his face with Luke Skywalker from the *Star Wars* movies. Remembering his name is easy after that! I use this approach all the time and find it very helpful.

Lastly, if someone tells you his or her name and you can't hear it or the pronunciation of it is difficult, just ask the person to repeat it. No one will think less of you for that. Actually, the opposite probably will occur. The person will think more of you because you wanted to make sure you heard the name correctly—it was important to you. Sometimes you can't hear, and it's not your fault. What is your fault is if you let that be the final outcome as to whether you learn someone's name or not. You may even have to ask the person to spell the name if it's odd enough—do whatever it takes.

I work in a field where I meet people from different parts of the world. Some of these people have names that are difficult to pronounce. Many times, I've had to ask them to repeat their names several times before I was able to pronounce the names myself. Occasionally, I have them spell out their names to help me remember. I do whatever is necessary to make sure I know their names the next time we meet. They understand that they are in a different country and their names are different than most people we meet. I've found that they will happily assist us in learning their names and will greatly appreciate the additional effort we put in to do so.

Don't say, "I'm bad at remembering names." Remember how we talked about the power of our words? If we say we're bad at remembering names and believe what we say, then we *will* be bad at remembering names. Even if we ignored the spiritual laws at play, we give ourselves an out from a natural standpoint. If we accept that we're not as good at remembering names as we want to be and give up, we don't give ourselves a chance to get better. Don't do that to yourself! It would be much better for you to constantly say, "I'm getting better at remembering names" and then make it a priority to do so.

22

Motivating People

When I talk about motivating people, what I'm really saying is getting someone to do something. The something doesn't matter; it could be anything. It could be selling a vacuum to a customer. It could be getting your kids to clean their rooms or getting an employee to do a better job at work. The principle behind getting someone to do something in all three cases is the same.

Most people we ever meet are chiefly concerned with their own wellbeing, so if we want to motivate them to do something, we're going to have to show them why it's in their best interest to do it. The more vivid we can paint that picture, the easier it is to get their cooperation. If you spend thirty minutes telling people they should do something because it's best for *you*, you're fighting an uphill battle. More on this later in the chapter.

Les Giblin, author of *Skill With People*, talked about the significance of finding out what's important to a person and then using that to motivate the individual. He said, "When you know *what* will move a person, you then know *how* to move them." There are two kinds of "whats" that will move someone: carrots (something a person wants) and sticks (punishment).

Using a carrot to motivate someone takes a little more effort, but it's the best form of long-term motivation. Our goal should be mental buy-in from the people we want to motivate, and the only way to get that is if they are bought in to the overall plan and *know* that it's in their best interest to follow that plan. Once they can see why it's in their best interest and know that if they follow the plan, they will get a carrot at the end, they now are their own source of motivation. Constantly trying to motivate someone else can be exhausting—we don't want to be in that game.

We can see companies regularly using carrots such as pay raises, bonuses, peer appreciation awards, or career ladders. All of these are carrots to give the employees something to shoot for. In and of themselves, these are not sufficient enough to make your company the best place to work, but they are an important step in the right direction. You might be thinking, "I'm paying people a salary, so they should give 100 percent all of the time." I agree, they should—especially if they are Christians, because Paul taught us (in Colossians 3:23, NKJV), "And whatever you do, do it heartily, as to the Lord and not to men." In reality, though, this isn't the case for a lot of people. Try getting rid of pay raises, bonuses, your career advancement path, and your culture of appreciation and see how it works out. People need carrots.

Did you know that Jesus had a carrot? It's written in Hebrews 12:2 (NKJV), "looking unto Jesus, the author and finisher of our faith, who for the joy that was set before Him endured the cross, despising the shame, and has sat down at the right hand of the throne of God." The joy that was set before Jesus was the opportunity to establish a New Covenant with God through His death. Jesus looked to this carrot to keep focused and motivated in the midst of unspeakable circumstances. We can do the very same thing as Christians to keep us motivated. Just like Jesus, we can be fully conscious of the future joy that is set before us: an eternity with God!

In 1 Corinthians 9:24–25 (NKJV), Paul wrote: "Do you not know that those who run in a race all run, but one receives the prize? Run in such a way that you may obtain it. And everyone who competes for the prize is temperate in all things. Now they do it to obtain a perishable crown, but we for an imperishable crown." Another carrot Christians pursue is an imperishable crown. Paul isn't talking about earning your salvation—Jesus bought that for you with His blood. Paul simply is talking about conducting ourselves in such a way that we fulfill God's call on our lives and are aware that our actions today have an impact on eternity. We want to win our "race" while we are here on the earth.

A stick (punishment) also can be an effective motivator, though not for sustained results. Punishment might work in the short term, but it has negative effects on relationships—I wouldn't make it my primary form of motivation. Most people absolutely will do what you want in order to avoid punishment, but you typically don't get their best effort, and you also create a barrier between you and that person. When punishment is your primary form of motivation, people are only going to do just enough to avoid punishment—why would they do anymore than that?

I served in the United States Army from 1994 to 1998. When we talk about organizations that are built upon using punishment as a motivator, this has to be at the top of the list. With every order, there is an implied, "If you don't do it, you're going to be in a world of hurt." The entire system is based on punishing people if they don't do the right thing. Do you want to know what happened? Just like you may have guessed, people tended to only do the right thing when someone was around giving them instructions on what to do next. When someone in authority wasn't around, soldiers literally would do nothing. What was their motivation to do the right thing when no one was watching? Many of them weren't serving more than one enlistment and didn't care about a long-term career. There were zero carrots and, as a result, soldiers did the bare minimum to avoid getting in trouble.

I don't live in a fantasyland. I recognize that, at some point, you'll need to use punishment as a motivator—there has to be a catch-all for people who are motivated no other way. People still have a core job to do within your organization. They have to meet their objectives. If people are unwilling to do that, then they might not be in the right job, or they might have to be retrained or let go. We should want to do everything in our power to help them before resorting to punishment, though. Punishment should be a last resort after all other options have been tried.

FIND OUT WHAT'S IMPORTANT TO A PERSON

Not all carrots are the same to all people. What motivates one person may not have any effect on another. Our job, if we want to effectively motivate people, is to find out what's important to each person and then use that as motivation to accomplish the goals of the team. In order to figure out what it's going to take to motivate people, we're going to have to spend time getting to know them. (I told you it was going to take a little more work, but it's worth it in the long run.)

Don't always assume money is the only thing people are interested in. Yes, it's important, but it's only one ingredient in their "happiness stew." Regardless of what we pay people (within reason), if we have a toxic people environment based on punishment as the primary motivator, people will just flat-out leave. This is especially true if we work with highly skilled people. If we mistreat people with a very marketable skill set, why would they stay at our company—especially if they could walk down the street and get a job at some other company that might treat them with trust and respect (and pay them what they are worth)?

In the software industry, one of the perks that I most appreciate is the ability to work remotely (away from the office). Because that perk is so valuable to me, I'm extra motivated to show I can continually meet my objectives. By doing so, there is no reason to question me when I'm working away from the office. Telecommuting is a carrot for me. For others, they may not even like being away from the office, so it has no effect on them as a motivator. For me, it's *huge* and has nothing to do with money—I'm still paid the same amount.

Find out what's important to the people around you and then do whatever you can to help set them on a path toward achieving both team goals and personal goals. Some people have personal career goals, and those are most important to them. Maybe they want to be doing a specific type of work. Maybe they want to get into management. Whatever it is, that's going to be what it takes to get the best out of those people. We can use the exact same approach with our kids. "You want to play video games at 8:00? Well, here's what you need to do in order to be able to do that." People are much more effective workers when they are working toward something they want.

As an example, let's say that someone wants to eventually become a manager of a small team within your company or church. He feels like he has a knack for it, and you see glimmers of it in him, as well. What you could do is sit down with him and create a road map of specific tasks that would get him closer to his objective. Perhaps you could delegate some of your management tasks to him. Maybe you could find small projects for him to lead. The point is, if you can move him closer to where he wants to go, he will be happier and more productive in his current role because he will see a light at the end of the tunnel. Besides, we don't want people to continue working in positions they don't like anyway—we won't get their best. Putting people in positions they want to be in is one of the best ways to keep them motivated and producing at a high level.

By now, I suspect someone is asking, "What, are we supposed to just move everyone around and eventually have no one left on our team?" I have never seen it play out that way—ever. People understand why they were hired and what they were hired to do. If they want to be in a completely different field, they'll leave to pursue that field. What I'm talking about here is giving them opportunities related to their current field of work or related to what your organization already does. If an employee is a graphic designer and wants to try his hand at web design, why not let him (if your company also does this kind of work)? Perhaps he'll find out he doesn't like it, and then he won't have to wonder anymore if that type of work is right for him. No harm done, and you didn't lose an employee. Maybe, though, you'll find out he really *is* good at it, and you now have an additional skill set on your team. Perhaps he is a better web designer than a graphic designer. In that case, you may want to move him to that team full time because it's better for both the company and the individual. It's a win-win! Sure, maybe you have to find another graphic designer, but your company is now stronger because you have a talented, motivated person in the correct position.

Volunteering at our local church is no different. People have hopes, dreams, and callings there just as they do at a job. If someone is volunteering on the worship team but feels like she also is being called to teach, work with her to develop a plan for getting her more exposure in that area. This way, you still can keep her on the worship team *and* find out if she is cut out for teaching. This keeps volunteers plugged in because they are encouraged to pursue God's plan for their lives while, at the same time, filling a need at your church.

"Hope deferred makes the heart sick, but a dream fulfilled is a tree of life" (Proverbs 13:12, NLT). If people are denied their hopes or dreams for too long, we may end up losing them altogether. I do not know many people who continually will serve year after year in an area they aren't satisfied with. Let's make sure we know where our volunteers want to be and do our best to get them there. Don't assume everyone is mature enough to wait on God for direction.

TALK ABOUT WHY IT'S BENEFICIAL TO THE OTHER PERSON

I want you to imagine for just a moment that you're a salesman and this is your main sales pitch when trying to sell your product: "I want you to buy this product, so I can get a big, fat commission." Sounds kind of silly, right? Do you think it's going to work? Of course not, because you haven't told the other person why it's in his best interest to buy your product. What's in it for him?

This exact same principle comes into play when we are trying to motivate someone to do something. We need to talk about why it's beneficial for the other person to do what we're asking. If we can do this effectively, we won't have to twist anyone's arm or beg—the person willingly will do it because he will see how it benefits him.

All too often, we approach people from a this-is-why-I-need-you-to-do-it standpoint. If we don't have any direct leverage over someone (such as a paycheck), this approach doesn't work very well. People aren't primarily motivated by what *we* want. They are motivated by what *they* want. As adults, each of us could come up with a laundry list of people who want stuff from us. How are we any different from the rest of them?

If you want people to come in and volunteer at a church function, what reason could you give them? What's in it for them? Here is an example of a self-focused approach: "We have a men's breakfast coming up and need some food servers. Contact Jim if you're interested." Now, here is an example of an others-focused approach: "We expect a large turnout at the upcoming men's breakfast with many first-time attenders. This is going to be a great opportunity to minister to them, strengthen them, and in turn strengthen their families. Part of making the experience positive for them is fast, efficient serving of the breakfast. If you want to make a tangible impact on the event, please contact Jim." Get the focus off of what *you* need and onto how it can benefit the potential volunteers (and the people who will attend).

If you want to share the gospel with someone, do you think the most effective way to do it is by saying, "God wants you saved, so come over here and I'll pray for you"? For some people, they don't know God from the guy down the street who works at the convenience store, so that's probably not going to work very well. The Holy Spirit draws people to God, yes, but we have a part to play, as well—we most definitely can make our delivery unappealing and uninspired. Remember, you and God are a team! A much better approach would be to talk about the personal benefits of being born again such as becoming a son or daughter of God and receiving His promises, the forgiveness of their sins, and their eventual place in heaven. The word "gospel" literally means "good news" and it's for a reason—a person would be crazy not to be born again after hearing it! If we're not sharing all of the benefits of being born again with unbelievers, we're missing one of the key ways to motivate them—by telling them why it's beneficial for them to receive God's gift. Always talk in terms of what your target audience wants, and you'll find it much easier to get other people's support.

23

Dealing with Conflict

Author Robert Bolton summed it up perfectly: "To be human is to experience conflict." If you are alive, and if you're around other people, you will have nearly limitless opportunities to experience conflict. The *Merriam-Webster Dictionary* defines conflict as:

> *conflict: mental struggle resulting from incompatible or opposing needs, drives, wishes, or external or internal demands*

Simply put, when we have problems with people, we experience conflict.

Here's the deal. Completely avoiding all conflict is impossible. Regardless of whether we think we are doing everything right on our end, we still are going to run into problems because we can't control other people. Unless we want to move up into the mountains of Montana, we have two choices: We either get good at managing the conflict in our lives, or we have it adversely affect our quality of life. There are no other options.

Remember the video game "boss" analogy I used in chapter 1? Well, that same concept applies to dealing with conflict. We can try to run away from conflict our whole lives, or we can meet it head-on and "defeat" it. If we let someone's difficult personality dictate the decisions we make (where we work, live, etc.), that person has now set the bar for the most difficult temperament we can handle. From here on out, that type of personality is going to have more control over us than it should. Do not live this way, or you'll end up having to play the "level" over again. Defeat your boss and level up!

Conflict can come in many forms: disagreements, arguments, personality conflicts, and even physical altercations (to name just a few). Not all conflict is bad, though. For instance, many disagreements are perfectly healthy and should be a part of our daily interactions, especially at the workplace. Civil disagreements are the foundry for great ideas and help bring to light deficiencies in current practices. A workplace without welcomed disagreements is probably not a very fun place to work because it means people don't feel empowered to disagree, usually because of fear. Disagreements (even heated ones) can be valuable as long as they are not left unresolved.

Unresolved conflict will poison any atmosphere—home, work, or volunteer. We are being carnal (relating to the physical world) when we are in a state of conflict. In Galatians 5:19–20 (NKJV), Paul wrote, "Now the works of the flesh are evident, which are: adultery, fornication, uncleanness, lewdness, idolatry, sorcery, hatred, contentions, jealousies, outbursts of wrath, selfish ambitions, dissensions, heresies." Paul warned us to stay as far away as possible from the activities he listed and it's for a reason—they'll open the door to more problems in our lives. It's the exact opposite of walking in the Spirit, which is what we all are instructed to do as Christians.

I want to point out again how much personal control we have over the quality of our own lives. If we choose to be in a perpetual state of conflict with everyone around us, is that God's fault? Absolutely not! *We* are deciding to participate in the conflict and, in many cases, to pour gasoline on the fire. Is it God's fault if we can't keep our big, fat mouths closed? No, it's not. In fact, He's already told us in dozens of places in His Word to pay close attention to what we say. He's already warned us. It's just a shame that people will destroy their lives with their own actions and words and then blame God for their circumstances. How unfair is that!

Let's say you were camping, and you discovered there were a bunch of poisonous snakes in some high grass. You notice that a fellow camper, a friend, is about to walk into the grass, so you yell out: "Hey, don't go in there! There are poisonous snakes in that grass—I've seen them myself!" What if your friend went in there anyway, ended up getting bitten, and then had the audacity to say that you didn't care about him (or that you wanted him to get bitten)? You'd be thinking: "What is wrong with this person? I told him not to go into the grass, and he completely ignored me!" Well, the same thing happens to God all day long. He's already told us to avoid certain activities because they're dangerous. If we choose to ignore Him and continue ahead into the danger zone, it's our own fault. Deuteronomy 30:19 (NKJV) sums it up perfectly: "I call heaven and earth as witnesses today against you, that I have set before you life and death, blessing and cursing; therefore choose life, that both you and your descendants may live." Make the choices that lead to life and blessings!

NEVER ARGUE

> *The start of a quarrel is like a leak in a dam, so stop it before it bursts.*
>
> —*Proverbs 17:14 (MSG)*

When I talk about arguing, I'm not talking about a civil exchange of opposing viewpoints. Instead, I'm talking about those times when we see red, emotions have taken over, and we lose control of our logic and reasoning. Google defines argument as:

> **argument:** *an exchange of diverging or opposite views, typically a heated or angry one*

This type of interaction usually is fueled by anger and results in hurt feelings and sometimes irreparable damage to relationships. In my adult life, I've had a few of these interactions with people. I can say without a doubt that I've regretted every single one of them, so much so that if I'm ever able to build a time machine, I plan to go back in time and prevent myself from engaging in them! I've had some arguments with my wife over the past twenty-one years that we've been married, and

I always end up having to apologize for how I acted. It's embarrassing and not something I'd ever be proud of at any point in my life. What have I learned? Do not argue. Avoid arguments at all costs.

Arguments create barriers and cannot be won. So much collateral damage can be caused in a heated argument that even if you somehow present a stronger logical case for your point of view, the amount of long-term goodwill you lose from the other person makes your "victory" completely hollow and worthless. Sure, you may have made your point, but guess what—you also lost a friend or put a wedge between yourself and your spouse. Was it worth it?

When we are angry, we are tempted to lose that filter that keeps us from saying things we know we'll regret later. Without this filter in place, we are at the mercy of our emotions, and that is a bad place to be. Our first response to anger often is to want to retaliate and hurt another person. We could say mean, hurtful, and destructive things. Once spoken, those things cannot be taken back. If we don't stop ourselves, we will sow a lot of "death" into our lives with our mouths that *will* come back to haunt us later.

Alcoholics Anonymous teaches a warning system called HALT. Each letter in HALT stands for a physical or emotional condition:

Hungry
Angry
Lonely
Tired

Whenever we are experiencing one of these feelings, we are the most vulnerable to making poor decisions. Recovering addicts are more likely to relapse during these times. Try to avoid making any important decisions or engaging in a heated discussion when you are hungry, angry, lonely, or tired. Instead, cool down, get something to eat, and perhaps sleep on it before you decide what to do.

If you feel an argument coming on, flat-out refuse to take part in it, if possible. Remove yourself from the situation if you have to! If you can't because of your position (pastor, manager, etc.), be really cautious here because it's very hard to listen to someone else unload on you without becoming emotionally stirred up yourself. You'll have to be strategic with what you say to not make the situation any worse. Plan to listen and ask questions to get to the root of the problem. You might have to control yourself through pure force of will! If you can, tell the person you want to have the conversation when things have cooled down. Do whatever you have to do to avoid making the situation any worse. "Fools vent their anger, but the wise quietly hold it back" (Proverbs 29:11, NLT). Don't be a fool; control your anger and your mouth.

ADMIT YOUR MISTAKES AND APOLOGIZE, IF NECESSARY

Each of us is wrong on occasion. What separates the mature from the immature is how we handle the situation when it happens. Do we use the situation to gain influence with the people around us, or do we lose some of their respect? Believe it or not, we actually can make mistakes and come out looking better for it by applying the following principles. It will require us to swallow our pride, but those who do so are the types of people whom others like to associate with.

If you're wrong, just admit it. You know you're wrong. Odds are others know you're wrong, too. Believe it or not, people respect you more when they see you mess up and admit it. It shows that you, too, are not perfect, and you're willing to improve. The longer you go without admitting it, the more damage you are doing to yourself in the eyes of the people around you. Nobody likes to be around someone who is so full of themselves (prideful or self-righteous) that they won't admit when they're wrong. In my opinion, it's the sign of an immature person. Mature people humble themselves and confess the fact that they miss it sometimes.

If we're wrong all the time, we have a different kind of problem altogether. Just like people don't like it if we never admit our mistakes, they also don't like it if we're wrong all the time—they lose confidence in our judgment. If you're wrong all the time, there is a reason. Maybe you're in the wrong position in your organization. Maybe you just need more training or time under your belt in your current position.

People will give you some leeway if you're coming up to speed in an area, but they eventually will expect you to positively contribute without having to second-guess everything you say. Maybe you just need to talk less or think more about what you could say before you say it.

It's OK if you're not perfect. Some people seem to think that it's some sort of unforgivable sin to be wrong. It isn't; it's called being human. Our goal is to continually drive those mistakes out of our lives, but there always will be some situations in which we say or do the wrong thing—it's just a part of life. Don't put such a heavy burden on yourself that you think you have to be correct 100 percent of the time—you don't. You are your own worst critic. Nobody is keeping a list of the number of times you've made mistakes—only you are.

When you make a mistake (and you will), I find it helpful to think about it this way: What did I learn from it, and what can I do to prevent it from happening in the future? If I learn from my mistake, I've come out a better person on the other side. This actually is very encouraging and takes some of the sting out of the mistake itself. If you are constantly trying to grow yourself and do new things, making mistakes is part of the game. If you never make any mistakes, it may mean you are continually operating in an area you are comfortable in and there probably isn't much room left in that space for personal growth. Get out into some new areas! Don't let mistakes discourage you from growing.

The second principle we can apply when we make a mistake is to follow up our confession with an apology, if necessary. If you need to apologize, just do it. Don't make excuses. Don't try to blame it on someone else. If you've done something wrong to someone, sincerely apologize and move on. Mature people don't make excuses for their failings—they own them and do whatever is in their power to make it right. Don't let things linger for months or years—that causes too many unneeded problems in the meantime.

The longer we go without apologizing, the worse things get. If our mistakes have slighted others in some way, the longer we go without apologizing means the more time there is for things like gossip to occur. What we don't want to happen is for people to start going around and saying potentially damaging things about us to others—all because we didn't apologize. Don't give the devil anything to work with. I have found that people actually are incredibly forgiving. If I acknowledge I did something wrong and ask for their forgiveness, they are pretty good about forgiving me and moving on. Will everyone act that way? No. A lot of people will, however, and that helps to make it easier to apologize as quickly as possible.

ASK QUESTIONS

In chapter 15, I had talked about how powerful asking questions can be as an alternative to telling people they are wrong. I need to talk a little more in this chapter about the value of asking questions with regards to dealing with and avoiding unnecessary conflict.

You might be surprised how effective a couple of well-thought-out questions can be at guiding people to their own mistakes while avoiding any sort of person-to-person conflict. I'm *not* saying we should avoid correcting people. I'm saying *how* we do it makes all the difference. In many cases, asking questions like "What are your plans if situation X pops up?" are much better than the alternative "Your plan doesn't address all of the problems. It won't work." The second statement creates a defensive atmosphere and is just asking for problems between people.

Even if you *know* something is wrong or there is a better way to do a particular thing, it still pays to ask questions. Remember, you more than likely learned the right way after doing it the wrong way first, too. Have some patience with the people around you and show them some grace. There are exceptions, but typically we have plenty of time to invest in creating a healthy atmosphere for helping others to see mistakes without creating conflict between each other.

If you're that guy who constantly tells people they are wrong, you're wasting a lot of potential influence with people—especially if you're usually right! What I mean is, if you are very capable at whatever you do, just think how effective you could be with that knowledge and a newfound ability to guide people to a solution while avoiding conflict. You'd become a superhero whom others would seek out for guidance because not only would you help them to see a better way of doing things, you would do it in a way that allows them to keep their dignity.

People who already respect your ability now would respect the way in which you help others and your organization to accomplish goals without alienating people. This is exactly how we expand our influence with others and open up new doors of opportunity for ourselves.

IF YOU HAVE A PROBLEM WITH SOMEONE, GO TALK TO THAT PERSON

What do you think is the "normal" or most common way people deal with conflict? I'd say it's avoidance and passive-aggressive retaliation (indirect resistance), based on personal observation. When people problems arise, many will try to avoid those with whom they have a problem as much as possible. If they have to be around the offenders, they may withdraw and keep those people at arm's length, denying them of any of the benefits of a healthy relationship. This is an ineffective way of managing a problem. Some people may say everything is OK, even when it's not. In fact, the people experiencing conflict may be openly hostile toward the offenders when they're not around and may even go so far as to try to sabotage the targets of their anger both personally and professionally. Instead of wasting all of that energy and incurring all of the stress associated with managing a bad relationship, I have a better idea: Go talk to the person.

If you have a problem with someone, go talk to that person. Don't talk to other people *about* that person. Don't create some sort of elaborate scenario in your head of how you are going to avoid that person for the rest of your life—just go talk face-to-face. Like a little weed that starts to grow in your garden, it's much easier to go pluck that thing out when it's one inch high than when it's five feet high. Some people let a little misunderstanding grow so big that they need heavy equipment to dig the sucker out. Don't let that happen! Deal with it swiftly and appropriately, and you'll discover that many major problems will never even materialize.

If you feel you can't resolve something face-to-face because you don't like direct confrontation, my question is: Why? If you feel physically threatened, that's a good reason. However, could it be because you're too prideful and don't want to admit you're wrong? Or, is it because you don't really want to resolve the problem—you'd rather make demands, accusations, or assume the worst about the person? If we are unable to resolve a problem face-to-face, we most definitely should *not* try to handle the issue through some other back channel, as our judgment already is suspect at that point. It's probably best to just forgive the person and move on.

Do not try to "resolve" significant misunderstandings via e-mail, text, or any other sort of one-sided communication method. To be blunt, this is what a coward would do. Misunderstandings are only resolved through healthy, person-to-person communication. Sending a one-sided message, so you can say exactly what you want without giving the other person a chance to respond in real time, is not fair to the other person and will backfire on you. To this day, I have *never* seen this work out like the sender apparently thinks it will. How do you know the other person even received the message? And if he did receive it, how do you know he even read it?

With one-sided communication, what typically happens is the recipient feels like he's being attacked, which probably was the intent of the person who sent it in the first place. This type of behavior is the exact opposite of what we should be trying to do, which is to resolve the conflict and remove that source of friction from our lives.

In Proverbs 6:16–19, there is a list of seven things that the Lord *hates*. Not dislikes. Not can mostly live with. *Hates!* Do you know what the last one is? It's "one who sows discord among brethren" (NKJV). God *hates* it when people instigate and perpetuate disagreements and contention among the church body. Do not have a hand to play in this! Do the opposite, which is to proactively seek to restore relationships and deal with problems as soon as they happen, while they are small. Don't pull the pin on a hand grenade by playing mind games with the intention of punishing the other person, because you're typically the one who ends up paying the highest price in the end. We'll talk about forgiveness later in this chapter.

Jesus gave us instructions on how to effectively deal with conflict between people. Here are three simple, guiding principles we can use to help us:

1. Do it quickly.

> *Therefore if you bring your gift to the altar, and there remember that your brother has something against you, leave your gift there before the altar, and go your way. First be reconciled to your brother, and then come and offer your gift. Agree with your adversary quickly, while you are on the way with him, lest your adversary deliver you to the judge, the judge hand you over to the officer, and you be thrown into prison.*
> —Matthew 5:23–25 (NKJV)

Jesus taught us that if we have any sort of issue with a fellow believer or an adversary, to immediately stop what we are doing and go be reconciled (restored) to that person. He warned us that if we don't, the problem could escalate out of control.

2. Meet in private (face-to-face).

> *Moreover if your brother sins against you, go and tell him his fault between you and him alone. If he hears you, you have gained your brother.*
> —Matthew 18:15 (NKJV)

After you have made it a priority to deal with the issue, go talk to the individual in private to try to work it out. It's important to resolve the problem between only you and the other person because we don't want the issue to grow legs and spread through gossip. If you do resolve the problem quickly, no one will ever know there was an issue in the first place. Many problems can be stopped cold in their tracks by just working through them together, face-to-face. Don't let fear keep you from doing the right thing, either.

3. Get help, if needed.

> *But if he will not hear, take with you one or two more, that "by the mouth of two or three witnesses every word may be estab-*

> lished." *And if he refuses to hear them, tell it to the church. But if he refuses even to hear the church, let him be to you like a heathen and a tax collector.*
> —Matthew 18:16–17 (NKJV)

After an initial, face-to-face meeting, if the person still is unwilling to resolve the issue, we are instructed to take one or two more witnesses with us to help reason with the person. To be most effective, these witnesses should be unbiased moderators, so the person won't feel like he is being attacked. If that *still* doesn't work, then our last step would be to bring it to the church. This could involve doing something like getting the pastor of your church to hear the disagreement and to suggest how it should be handled. If the person (assuming *he* is the source of the problem) still insists on perpetuating the conflict with you, the only option you have left is to forgive him, apologize for any wrongdoing on your part, and limit your contact with him, if necessary.

Those three principles could save all of us a whole lot of pain and misery because they are designed to deal with a problem while it's small and new—when it's easiest to address. Don't just use these principles when you're dealing with Christians, either—use them with every relationship in your life. Sure, you probably won't bring your unsaved neighbor to your pastor, but you most certainly can implement the other steps in the process above to prevent any conflict from growing out of control.

It's good to remember, too, whom the instructions came from—Jesus! We'd be wise to do what He said.

CHOOSE NOT TO BE OFFENDED

You always get to choose how you respond to circumstances in your life, and no one can ever take that away from you. Unlike animals, humans have God's law written in their hearts (Romans 2:15) and don't have to be dominated by their natural impulses. Regardless of what someone says or does, you get to decide exactly how to respond to it—even under stress. Figure 7 is a visual representation of what I

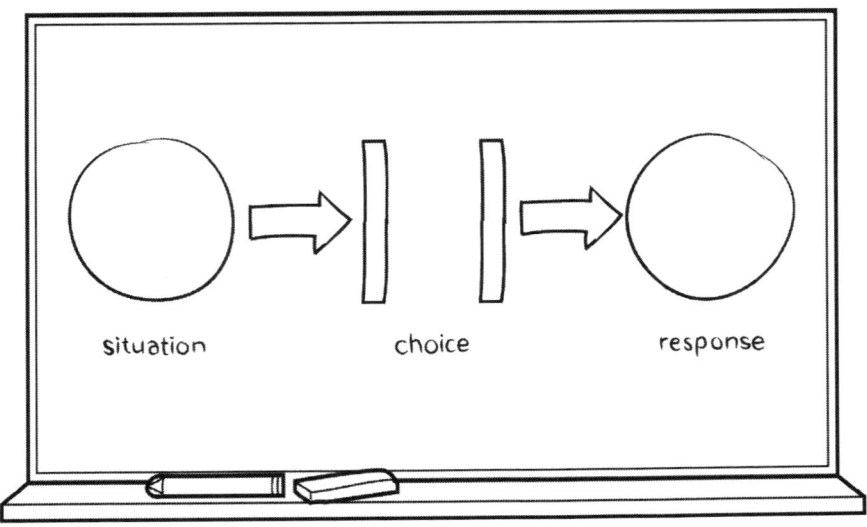

Figure 7

am talking about.

If another person says something to you, and you get offended and make a poor, hasty decision because of it, you have no one else to blame but yourself. No one can make you take offense to something—you choose to be offended. I know that's hard for some people to hear because they've been operating like they've had no choice for most of their lives. Part of living a happier, more successful life is understanding that our reactions to circumstances are completely within our control. We can read in 2 Timothy 1:7 (NIV), "For the Spirit God gave us does not make us timid, but gives us power, love and self-discipline." If we use self-discipline to control our responses to situations in our lives, we will make more good decisions, and those good decisions will affect us in a more positive way.

People often get offended and leave a church because of something someone else said or did. Maybe the pastor said something they disagree with in a sermon. Perhaps one of the people they know at the church said something hurtful about them to someone else. Instead of properly resolving the conflict with the person, they feel like they have to leave—more to show their disapproval than because the situation calls for their exit. It's another form of passive-aggressive behavior.

I've seen people come to church whose lives are a mess. With God's help, they turn things around and get moving in the right direction. Then, all of a sudden, they just aren't there anymore—sometimes after years of faithful attendance. Come to find out, they got offended over some situation within the church and left. It's like they totally forgot where they used to be and how far God has brought them! People do this all the time—they choose to take offense and, as a result, end up making decisions that negatively impact their long-term happiness and success.

Wherever there are people, there are opportunities to be offended. Unless we plan to live on a deserted island for the rest of our lives, the better we are at dealing with offense, the more successful we're going to be in life. I'm not for one minute condoning offensive behavior, I'm just not going to let it affect my family and me in a negative way. Why would I give someone else that much control over my life? As Christians, we should have one Lord—Jesus (Ephesians 4:4–6)! If we let people influence our lives through offense, we are no longer being led by the Spirit of God. Instead, we are being led by other people—and who knows what's leading them?

Don't let offensive people or situations dictate how far you can go in life. If we are going to leave organizations and walk away from friendships every time someone says or does something offensive, we are choosing to exempt ourselves from reaching the highest levels of success in our lives. We also are limiting our ability to help others. The higher we go in life, the bigger of a target we become. If we choose to take offense at the drop of a hat, we may as well forget about ever significantly influencing any sizable group of people, because eventually some (or all) of them are going to do things that could offend us—if we allowed it. Don't allow it.

Let's say for a minute that I was the enemy of all the Christians in the world and I was constantly looking for ways to divide and separate them, so they could never generate enough momentum to get anything significant done for the kingdom of God. How would I do that? Well, the first thing I'd do is try to keep them apart to begin with—try to give them reasons to not even come to church in the first place. If that failed, I'd try to get them to focus on things they don't like and pit them against each other, in hopes that some would get offended and leave. I'd definitely convince them they shouldn't give any money to the church, because I don't want it to grow. I'd tempt them to compare and judge each other behind their backs and to spread lies, in hopes of causing division. I'd plant thoughts in their heads to try to get them worked up over situations and convince them that they just have to do something about it—*right now!* "Someone was talking about *you*. *You* don't have to take it. *You* don't have to be here; you can just find another church. How dare someone say that about *you!*" Does that sound like God to you? To me, that sounds like someone trying to get you worked up so you'll make an irrational decision—one that will probably hurt you in the long run.

What I just described is exactly what is happening in the church all over the world today! Refuse to take part in this game! It is not a sin to be tempted; it's a sin to act on the temptation. We all have thoughts come to us, and not all of them are good.

We are told (in 2 Corinthians 10:4–5, NKJV), "For the weapons of our warfare are not carnal but mighty in God for pulling down strongholds, casting down arguments and every high thing that exalts itself against the knowledge of God, bringing every thought into captivity to the obedience of Christ." One of our spiritual weapons is the Word of God (Ephesians 6:17). Not only can we use God's Word to cut through deception, we also can use it as the measuring stick for our response to situations. When we know a potential response to a situation runs contrary to God's Word, we don't even have to think about it—we can just reject it. We can use the Word of God for casting down arguments and bringing every thought into captivity. When you are being tempted with thoughts of being offended, and you're not sure how to handle it, I encourage you to find out what God says about your situation and use that as your foundation for approaching it. (Tables 1, 2, and 3 include examples of what I am talking about.) Just ask yourself, "What does God say about it?" Thinking this way sure makes life a lot easier.

Opportunity to Take Offense
"Hey, Jill is saying you're [insert untrue statement] to other people at the church."

What God Says
Moreover if your brother sins against you, go and tell him his fault between you and him alone. If he hears you, you have gained your brother. —Matthew 18:15 (NKJV) *And see to it that your conscience is entirely clear, so that every time you are slandered or falsely accused, those who attack or disparage your good behavior in Christ will be shamed [by their own words].* —1 Peter 3:16 (AMP) *Bless those who persecute you; bless and do not curse.* —Romans 12:14 (NKJV) *But I say to you who hear [Me and pay attention to My words]: Love [that is, unselfishly seek the best or higher good for] your enemies, [make it a practice to] do good to those who hate you, bless and show kindness to those who curse you, pray for those who mistreat you. Whoever strikes you on the cheek, offer him the other one also [simply ignore insignificant insults or losses and do not bother to retaliate—maintain your dignity]. Whoever takes away your coat, do not withhold your shirt from him either.* —Luke 6:27–29 (AMP)

Table 1

Opportunity to Take Offense
"I really don't agree with what Pastor Andy said about [insert subject]."

What God Says
Listen to counsel and receive instruction, that you may be wise in your latter days. —Proverbs 19:20 (NKJV) *These were more fair-minded than those in Thessalonica, in that they received the word with all readiness, and searched the Scriptures daily to find out whether these things were so.* —Acts 17:11 (NKJV) *Dearly loved friends, don't always believe everything you hear just because someone says it is a message from God: test it first to see if it really is. For there are many false teachers around.* —1 John 4:1 (TLB) *But test all things carefully [so you can recognize what is good]. Hold firmly to that which is good.* —1 Thessalonians 5:21 (AMP)

Table 2

Opportunity to Take Offense
Your worship leader says she is taking the ministry in a different direction and your service is no longer needed.

What God Says
Trust in the Lord with all your heart, and lean not on your own understanding; In all your ways acknowledge Him, and He shall direct your paths. —*Proverbs 3:5–6 (NKJV)*
"For I know the plans I have for you," declares the LORD, "plans to prosper you and not to harm you, plans to give you hope and a future." —*Jeremiah 29:11 (NIV)*
Roll your works upon the Lord [commit and trust them wholly to Him; He will cause your thoughts to become agreeable to His will, and] so shall your plans be established and succeed. —*Proverbs 16:3 (AMPC)*

Table 3

FORGIVE

As Christians, we are told to forgive other people—it's not an option. God did not say, "If it's convenient for you, please try to forgive people." In Matthew 18:21–22 (NKJV), we read: "Then Peter came to Him and said, 'Lord, how often shall my brother sin against me, and I forgive him? Up to seven times?' Jesus said to him, 'I do not say to you, up to seven times, but up to seventy times seven.'" Jesus wasn't literally saying to forgive someone 490 times—but not to on the 491st time! He was saying that we should forgive our brother as many times as necessary. There is no limit to how often we are expected to forgive.

There are no stipulations regarding forgiveness, either—if someone does you wrong, you forgive him or her.

After responding to Peter, Jesus told a story of a man who was indebted to a king for a great deal of money and could not repay it. The king was going to sell the man and his family into slavery to pay off the debt, but when the man begged for patience, the king was moved with compassion and forgave his debt. This same man then turned around and went to collect a smaller amount from a fellow servant who owed him money, but when the fellow servant begged for patience, he would not forgive him. The king found out about his behavior, was angered by his unwillingness to forgive as he had been forgiven, and had him thrown into prison to be tortured until his debt was paid.

Jesus used this parable to teach us at least a couple of things. The first thing is that we are like the man who was indebted to the king—we had created so much sin debt between us and God that there was no way we could pay it. Instead, God showed compassion on us and wholesale forgave us of it (sending Jesus to die for us as a substitute). The second thing is that we are *not* to act like the man, who refused to forgive the fellow servant, when we deal with other people in our lives. We have been forgiven of a great debt, so likewise we are expected to forgive people who have sinned against us. The amount others "owe" us pales in comparison to what we have been forgiven of, so we should freely and quickly forgive others of their "debt."

It seems like a lot of people think of forgiveness as letting someone off the hook—like you're saying to the other person, "What you did to me is OK, I forgive you." That is not what forgiveness is. When you forgive someone, you are not condoning the behavior. Instead, you are severing the cord between the offense and you—you no longer give it any power over you. You are releasing that person from any control or influence over you and are effectively washing your hands of the pain and hurt. You are letting go of it. Think of releasing a balloon into the air and just walking away—it's just gone, and it's not coming back. Forgiveness is a healthy way to deal with hurt without it destroying your life from the inside out.

Forgiving someone doesn't mean we have to be friends, either. Some people are confused and think that if they forgive someone, the relationship has to move forward as if the hurt or offense never took place. This is not true. Forgiving someone doesn't mean we pretend the bad thing never happened—that would be foolishness. If someone gave my underage kids alcohol while they were at his house, I'd forgive him but I wouldn't immediately let them go over to his house again—not as a punishment but as common sense. I'd forgive him to diffuse my anger, and then I would protect my kids from further misbehavior. You have to make the call whether the relationship is worth restoring and trust God to make that possible.

Let's not forget that some people truly are sorry about what they said or did to you. In these cases, verbally expressing your forgiveness can help to facilitate the healing process. Personally speaking, if someone does me wrong and apologizes for it, I try to make it a point to say, "I forgive you." People need to hear this because it is the most powerful way of saying, "I am no longer holding this against you."

Many people don't want to forgive, because they want revenge—they want the other person to feel as bad as they do. One question: How's that working out for you, so far? God told us not to take revenge, so if that's how you think, you should repent (turn from that way of thinking) and start doing things God's way. We can plainly read in Proverbs 20:22 (TLB): "Don't repay evil for evil. Wait for the Lord to handle the matter." Revenge only makes matters worse and doesn't fix the original problem. Sure, it might make us feel a little better for a moment, but the pain and anger still are there and will continue to build up again once our revenge fix has worn off. God told us to forgive because it's truly the only way to recover from the terrible things that happen to all of us.

Bottled-up hurts will completely eat us alive from the inside out. All of that pent-up hate, anger, and sadness *will* come out of us in some way—it has to. It's either going to come out as forgiveness, which is healthy, or it's going to manifest itself as health problems or destructive behavior. I have yet to meet someone who will not forgive people and is truly happy. Why? Because people who don't forgive are tormented inside. The unforgiveness is eating them up. They keep it all bottled up inside thinking that if they forgive the other person, he somehow wins. In reality, the other person probably doesn't spend one second thinking about what he said or did to them—they are the only ones affected. Any time you choose not to forgive someone, *you* are losing—not the person who did you wrong.

Whenever you choose not to forgive someone, it's like throwing a rock in a backpack you're carrying. You might be able to handle a few rocks, but after awhile, it becomes completely unmanageable. What's your only choice? Take the rocks out—forgive people! You can't run your race in life wearing a backpack full of rocks. You can decide to lighten your load by forgiving people.

Forgiveness isn't conditional, either—it doesn't depend on an apology first. If you're waiting for someone to apologize, you might be waiting for a *really* long time. In fact, I can almost guarantee you that some people will *never* apologize—they literally will die first. What then? Are we going to be forced to carry around that unforgiveness for the rest of our lives? That is why proactively forgiving people is so powerful! We don't need another person's apology to forgive him or her, all we need is to make the decision to do it. We are empowered to diffuse a situation without help from anyone else. This is why it's impossible to keep people down who operate in forgiveness on a continual basis—they refuse to put the rocks in their backpacks that would slow them down.

This is going to sound cold and callous, but give me a minute to explain. Nobody cares about your baggage. You know all of that hurt you've been carrying around for possibly years—that pain that has been internally tormenting you, keeping you up at night, giving you stomach problems, and poisoning all of the close relationships with men (or women) in your life? Nobody can possibly care about it as much as you do—they are too absorbed in themselves. The people who hurt you don't care, either. I care about your hurt only because I want to help you get rid of it. So why would you want to hold onto it?

When we die, there is no trophy awarded to the person who carried around the most hurt. It does not show strength to be able to live with truckloads of unforgiveness—it actually shows incredible weakness, especially if we're Christians. God will not commend us for our unforgiveness when we get to heaven. The only thing unforgiveness does is prevent us from living the happiest, most productive lives possible right now. We will never fully realize God's plan for our lives if we are unwilling to forgive people of their offenses.

Some really terrible things have happened to people. Horrible things. I'm not trying to trivialize or make light of them. All I'm trying to say is: What are our options? If something terrible happened to you, we can't build a time machine and go back to prevent it from happening. All we have is now. You can either deal with the problem or keep dragging it around and have it affect your future.

If you need help, get it. Ask God for help. Tell Him you want to forgive people but you don't know how because the hurt seems too big for you. If you're born again, He's your Father, He loves you, and He will help you. Seek help from a counselor at your church. If your church doesn't have one, find an external counselor. My point is you don't have to live with the hurt. Get help, if you need it. Jesus said (in Mark 10:27, NKJV), "For with God all things are possible." This includes helping you to forgive others.

24

Communication and Technology

With the continued rise of technology in every area of our lives, I felt it necessary to address the topic from a people-skills perspective. In a lot of ways, technology has made our lives better: easier access to information, online shopping, and instant access to our friends. In other ways, however, we have really taken a step backward as far as person-to-person interactions are concerned. In this chapter, I'm hoping to give you some helpful tips to guide your interactions when using technology to communicate with the people around you. In some cases, you may even want to avoid using technology altogether when working through an issue with another person because it can be limiting. Technology by itself is neither good nor bad—it's just a tool. If used properly, it can be powerful at reaching a vast amount of people quickly. Used improperly, it can create problems on a scale unimaginable.

EFFECTIVE COMMUNICATION RESULTS FROM HUMAN CONTACT

Humans communicate best when they are face-to-face. Sometimes that communication can be uncomfortable, but no technology can replace a person-to-person interaction when you want to get important business done. As a matter of fact, technology (such as endless e-mail threads or text messages) often can complicate interactions that may have taken only a few minutes in person. Many people have gotten rusty on their face-to-face, interpersonal-communication skills because of their over-reliance on electronic forms of communication. We need to realize that our most important interactions with people still happen when we are physically present with them. If we want those interactions to go well, we need to have fully operational communication skills.

In chapter 19, I talked about how important nonverbals (facial expressions, tone of voice, etc.) are when communicating. When we e-mail, text, and use other forms of electronic communication, we completely lose all of that nonverbal information. Have you ever gotten an e-mail from someone and wondered about the state of mind of the person who sent it—was the person happy, sad, or angry? This is because you can't assess the person using your other, more reliable senses. Instead, you have to depend on the written words of the sender, which may be poorly constructed to begin with.

Intent and context often can be lost when using electronic communication. I don't know how many times I've read and reread a text message before I've sent it, only to find out later that the interpretation of the one who received it was completely different than my intent. Sometimes, I've had to apologize because I didn't realize until later how the person could have misinterpreted my meaning. When we are face-to-face, we can pick up on facial expressions and, more importantly, ask questions and get answers in real time. If you have important business to do, do it in person, if possible. If that's not possible, then try an alternative like video conferencing where you can at least see the other person's face while communicating.

Humans are social beings, and intimate relationships are one of the key components of our happiness. Technology is a poor substitute for human contact. We may have *more* interactions with people, but the quality of those interactions typically is far less valuable than it used to be a short couple of decades ago without our electronics. Are your 1,548 Facebook (or whichever the current social media platform) "friends" really your friends? Technology has given us more acquaintances, but they are only that—acquaintances. A real, close relationship only can be nurtured by being physically present with a person (and even then, some people really struggle). Humans crave deep, personal connections—something more than just sharing videos of screaming goats, or cats getting their heads stuck in yogurt containers.

TECHNOLOGY MAKES US FEEL ANONYMOUS

Because of the anonymous nature of many technologies (multiplayer video games, user forums, product reviews, etc.), people will say things they *never* would say to a person face-to-face. Since we are physically separated from the people we are communicating with, some take that as a license to say any inappropriate thing that comes into their heads. This is totally unacceptable. Words are powerful regardless of what medium they are conveyed across. Do we think we can say whatever we want via technology and not have it affect our lives? We are to conduct ourselves the same regardless of our communication method—that's what mature people (and especially Christians) do.

It's nothing new for people to communicate differently through technology than they would face-to-face. Before the Internet, there was the telephone. Have you ever overheard people being rude to a phone solicitor or to customer support? I have. I remember doing it myself, too! I've repented! Many times, people who say they don't like confrontation can be extremely confrontational when they aren't in the same room with the other person. It's almost like we don't think of the guy on the other end of the phone as being real. This should not be the case.

The goal of every Christian should be to act consistently (patient, loving, encouraging, etc.) across every area of our lives at all times. There should be no difference between our behavior at work or at home. If we treat our co-workers with respect, we should also treat our spouses with respect. We should talk to people at the grocery store the same way we talk to our friends at church. From a technology standpoint, this means we should communicate the same using technology as we do face-to-face.

We should realize that God sees everything we do anyway. The author of Hebrews 4:13 (NKJV) wrote, "And there is no creature hidden from His sight, but all things are naked and open to the eyes of Him to whom we must give account." God's not holding sins against us, but it's not like we are getting away with anything.

THE INTERNET NEVER FORGETS

Assume when you press "send," whatever electronic communication you're sending will live forever. Never assume people will delete what you've just sent them. Never assume people will not forward what you've just sent them, even if you've asked them not to. And if you're posting something on a social media site, you may as well put it on the front page of a newspaper—because it's now out there for the entire world to see, even if you think only a few people can get to it.

The Internet never forgets. Once the message or picture has left your device, it is no longer in your control, and people can do whatever they want with it. People can share what you told them with everyone they know or copy it from a website to their computer and keep it forever. To make matters worse, companies that provide technology services (social media sites, etc.) keep a historical record of activity and even back up their data at regular intervals to make sure no one loses anything. This means that the picture of you doing something you shouldn't be doing now can be frozen in time and archived. Your text message history? Yup, your cell phone carrier saves that—and some carriers keep it for years. Yikes! In addition, companies get hacked, and people steal images and personal information. You really have no control over things you've sent.

There are eyes everywhere now, too, so it's more important than ever to live a godly life. Every cell phone is a set of eyes and ears that can potentially report on any compromising behavior. All it takes is one short video or picture to completely ruin your testimony (your ability to influence people as a Christian)—so be careful. I'm not trying to make you paranoid, I'm just pointing out the reality of the situation.

One of my past employers had this saying called "The Headline Test." It went something like this: "If you wouldn't feel comfortable having what you wrote as the headline of a newspaper article, then you shouldn't write it." I've heard others say, "If you would be embarrassed if your grandma read it, you shouldn't write it." This doesn't just go for words, it goes for any form of electronic communication. Err on the side of being overly protective of what you share, and you should be fine. Assume everything you say will go "viral" (spread like wildfire), and you should be good.

25

How Do We Get Better?

Jesus told us (in Luke 6:45, NKJV) that "A good man out of the good treasure of his heart brings forth good; and an evil man out of the evil treasure of his heart brings forth evil. For out of the abundance of the heart his mouth speaks." Change your heart; change how you speak (and act). Use this material and material like this to change your heart, so you can bring forth more good for yourself and others.

The apostle Paul said (in Romans 12:2, NKJV), "And do not be conformed to this world, but be transformed by the renewing of your mind, that you may prove what is that good and acceptable and perfect will of God." We, as Christians, should be constantly renewing our minds to the things of God. Understanding who we are in Christ will radically change us as people from the inside out. As our inside changes, we can't help but change on the outside, too. If we want to get better results with people, we also must renew our minds to better and more effective ways of communicating. I believe every Christian should be firmly established in the Word, led by the Spirit of God, *and* equipped with a set of practical skills for successfully handling interactions with others.

LOOK FOR OPPORTUNITIES

The only way to get better at a skill in life is to practice. Getting more skillful with people is no different. I've given you many concepts to play around with, but unless you get out there and do something with them (even add your own flavor to them), they aren't going to do you any good. If you stop at just knowing them, then you've effectively wasted all of the time you've spent reading this book. Don't do that to yourself—practice!

I don't know a single person who has no human interaction on a daily basis. What that means is most of us have plenty of opportunities to use the skills we've learned in this book. When you go to your favorite restaurant, learn the names of the employees who work there. When you're at church, smile more. The next time you're standing around the water cooler at work, ask someone what his name is and what he does for your company. The list could go on and on, but understand this is what it looks like in real life. Sure, we may occasionally have some really big wins with people, but most of our influence is going to be built up through all of the smaller interactions we have with people on a daily basis.

The next time you talk with someone, practice the listening skills we talked about. Run down a mental checklist before and during the conversation to remind yourself of what you could do differently. "Am I looking at the person in the eyes? Am I giving him a chance to finish speaking before I speak? Am I giving him vocal queues to show I'm listening?" Consistently doing these little things is how we become more skillful with people. You may not think you've accomplished anything, but the person will walk away thinking to himself—at least subconsciously—that was a good conversation. He will feel listened to because you sent the right signals while engaging with him. Again, if you want to be more skillful with people, this is how it plays out in your day-to-day interactions.

Don't use the skills you've learned only in a reactive way—use them proactively. Go out and find people. On your way out to lunch, ask the security guard if he wants anything while you're out. Most people won't ever do that, but we will. Even if he says, "No thanks," you now stand out to him. Most people walk by him and never say a single word, but now he'll remember you. We are Christians. We love people. Things like this are a pleasure to do because we want to help others experience better lives. Proactively build out your Opportunity Tree. Don't just play defense with these skills. Go on the offensive and consciously create stronger relationships with the people around you. You can have as many healthy connections with as many people as you'd like—there is no limit.

If you have a stressful relationship in your life, you have the perfect opportunity to apply some of the principles we have talked about. Maybe you need to start out small. Compliment the individual on something he or she has done recently. Have a quick conversation about how the person is doing. Or, maybe you need to apologize for your part in getting the relationship to the state it's at right now. Don't be a bystander in your own life! If relationships are weighing you down, do something about them. Maybe you didn't know how to go about it before, but I bet you have some options now. Use what you've learned to change the circumstances in your life.

CONTINUE LEARNING

All of the successful people I know (Christians and non-Christians) are lifelong learners—they never stop trying to grow themselves, both in the things of God and in fields that interest them. These people are always reading, taking classes, and exposing themselves to information they've never encountered before. They do this because they want to know a better way of doing things. They want to learn from the successes (or sometimes failures) of others in an attempt to apply that same information to their lives. They want to push their lives to the limit and make as big of a positive impact on others as possible.

As soon as we stop learning, we put a cap on our success. Stagnation is dangerous because we can end up being left behind. It's healthy to continually challenge our current ways of thinking. We're not the same people we were ten years ago, and concepts that were beyond us (or may have seemed irrelevant to us in the past) might make perfect sense to us now. Ongoing learning allows us to periodically update our understanding and knowledge in important subjects and glean applicable information for today. At a minimum, we should always be seeking out information on topics we know can have a positive impact on our lives (God, finances, marriage, leadership, etc.). When we stop learning, we stop growing.

It is my personal belief that we should always be reading at least one book at any given time (or listening to an audiobook)—not just any book, either, but something with "teeth" (information you can apply to your life). Pick a topic that interests you or that you're weak in, and just start going. This is one of the simplest things we can possibly do to keep growing. If we read for just twenty minutes a day, that would be more than 121 hours of reading a year. Over a decade, that would be more than 1,216 hours. That is an insane amount of learning, and we could get there by spending very little time reading each day!

Years ago, I read a book in which the author recommended listening to audiobooks and teachings while commuting to work. It seemed like a good idea at the time and has turned out to be one of the primary personal growth avenues in my life! My average commute to work is twenty minutes, so in a day, I can get in forty minutes of learning. That's 200 minutes per week and more than thirteen hours per month. I'm already trapped in my car, so it's not like I'm stealing time from any other area of my life—I'm simply using the time I have more effectively.

If you don't feel like you know as much of God's Word as you should, use your commuting time to grow yourself spiritually. Find Christian teachers you like and start feeding on their teachings as you drive back and forth to work. If an average sermon is thirty minutes, you can fit in five to ten additional sermons per week! With the technology we have today, you can load up dozens of teachings on your smartphone and grind through them all while you're in your car. Are you confused about how to be led by the Spirit of God? Get a teaching on it. Are you struggling with temptation in a certain area? Get a teaching on it. You can quickly go from being an uneducated Christian to being someone who has a deeper understanding of the Word of God—all by listening to teachings in the car.

Maturity does not automatically come with age. I've met sixty-year-olds who act like teenagers, and I've met twenty-year-olds who were wise far beyond their years. Just because someone is old, it doesn't mean they are wise. Maturity can be seen as fruit in your life and is irrefutable. If we're living from crisis to crisis and constantly torching all of the relationships in our lives, we might have to put on our "big-boy pants" and come to the conclusion that we are less mature in certain areas than we thought we were. Identify those areas and then grow!

SET UP SYSTEMS TO ENFORCE GOOD BEHAVIOR

If you're like me, it's easy to get overwhelmed with new information. You may read something, completely agree with what was said, but then never follow through with what you've learned. Sometimes this is because you just forget what you've read. It's hard to read a list of "the seventy-two principles for making your life better" and remember more than a couple. How can we make sure to take the information that we've learned and apply it to our lives, so we can get the results we want? One of the best ways I've found is to use tools I already have at my disposal to "force" me to do the things I've already identified as being valuable.

If you carry around a smartphone, you already have the perfect "nag machine." This little device can be set up to remind you to do activities that you would otherwise forget about. For example, if you think that inviting people to lunch is a good idea, why don't you set a reminder on your phone to take someone to lunch every week? Or, if you don't think you appreciate people enough, why not set an everyday reminder to go find someone who has helped you recently and appreciate him or her? This is one of the primary reasons our smartphones were created in the first place—to be a pocket calendar and personal assistant. Take advantage of that functionality to keep yourself on track.

In the past, I've used my computer-based work calendar to remind me to do specific beneficial activities. For example, I put a reminder on my calendar to go find someone each week to talk to and recognize something outstanding the person had done. Each week at the same time, a box would pop up while I was sitting at my computer to remind me to go and do the thing I already convinced myself I should be doing in the first place. Again, if we don't do the things we've talked about in this book, they won't do us any good—the action is what causes the result to manifest in our lives.

If you have a friend who is a learner like yourself, you can partner with him or her to help keep you on track. Get together periodically to check up on each other's progress and to encourage one another. If you keep the ideas at the forefront of your mind, you're more likely to act on them. You might be amazed by how much further you can take this information if you have a partner to help you along the way. In Proverbs 27:17 (NKJV), we can read, "As iron sharpens iron, so a man sharpens the countenance of his friend." Find someone who can sharpen you as a person in these areas. In return, you'll be able to sharpen him.

Conclusion

Well, you did it! You made it all the way to the end! I know we've covered a lot of material, but you now have the basics of what I believe every Christian should know to be effective at managing relationships and avoiding unnecessary strife. What we covered was not exhaustive by any means, but it can "stop the bleeding" in some of the areas where you may have been experiencing the same problems year after year.

I want to challenge you again to put the information into practice. Do your best to internalize what we covered and turn it from "head knowledge" to "heart knowledge." Adopt the principles as a new way of life so you can be more effective at home, at work, and at church. What we covered is meant to be applied everywhere.

You may have heard the saying, "You are the only Jesus some people will ever see." You might be the reason why someone will decide to give his life to the Lord or to turn his back on Him forever. You are God's representative while here on the earth. If you are offensive, mean, or standoffish, what kind of message does that send about the person you are representing?

I will continually pray for the eyes of your understanding to be enlightened, not only concerning spiritual wisdom and knowledge of God but also wisdom concerning how to best apply the information in this book to your life. We are a family. The stronger and healthier each member is, the more effective we will be as a whole. Wherever you are, I want you to be a living testimony for God to show others what a person walking out godly wisdom looks like. You will attract people, not only with your words but with your actions. Remember, with God all things are possible. There are no limits except the ones you place on yourself. Be blessed!

Afterword

I'd love to hear from you! If you liked the book, have any suggestions for how to make the material better, or would like to contact me about my availability as a speaker, instructor, or coach, you can reach me at:

Blog: www.effectivelivingllc.com/blog
E-mail: contact@effectivelivingllc.com

If you accepted the Lord (were born again) because of this book, I would *love* to hear from you! Each salvation makes a great testimony that can be shared with others. I will *never* share your personal information with *anyone*.

If you found this book valuable, I encourage you to share it with someone else. Loan it to a friend. Incorporate it into a small group at your local church. Submit an online review to compel others to read it, as well. Let's get this information out to as many fellow believers as possible. The stronger we are individually, the stronger we will be as a church body!

How to Be Born Again

You might be asking yourself, "What's with all this 'born-again' talk I keep hearing about?" Well, quite simply, there is something that prevents us from having a relationship with a perfect and holy God, and it's called sin. In Romans 3:23 (NKJV), we are told "for all have sinned and fall short of the glory of God." Every single person is guilty of violating God's divine law, and because of this, we can't have a relationship with Him—not now and not in heaven. No amount of good deeds can make up for this separation between us and God, either.

God's standard is perfection. Going to church doesn't make us good enough. Being a good person doesn't do it. Believing there *is* a God doesn't cut it, either—even the devil believes that (James 2:19)! Religion also doesn't fix the problem between God and man. Many times, religion actually makes it worse because it tries to convince you that you can work hard enough to get right with God—you can't. The apostle Paul said in Ephesians 2:8–9 (NKJV), "For by grace you have been saved through faith, and that not of yourselves; it is the gift of God, not of works, lest anyone should boast." What is this gift Paul talked about? Glad you asked—it's salvation through faith in Jesus!

God recognized that man never could fix the sin problem between us and Him, so He came up with a plan to fix it Himself. Paul said in Romans 6:23 (NKJV), "For the wages of sin is death, but the gift of God is eternal life in Christ Jesus our Lord." God adheres to a justice system He put in place, and someone has to pay the penalty of sin, which is death. His master plan for reconciling the world to Himself consisted of coming to Earth in the sinless person of Jesus, paying for our sins with His own blood (to satisfy the death requirement of sin), and offering this gift freely to anyone who wants it. And just like a gift that may be sitting down at the post office with your name on it, you need to go pick it up and say: "That's mine! I'll take that, please!"

In John 3, a man who recognized Jesus came from God met with

Him but apparently didn't know what to ask for. We read in John 3:3 (NKJV), "Jesus answered and said to him, 'Most assuredly, I say to you, unless one is born again, he cannot see the kingdom of God.'" In order to see heaven, Jesus said we have to be spiritually born again—we need to make the transition from spiritual death (the sin nature we were born with) to spiritual life (born of God).

Receiving this free gift of salvation is one of the easiest things you can do. In Romans 10:9–10, we are given very explicit directions for how to be born again. We are told "that if you confess with your mouth the Lord Jesus and believe in your heart that God has raised Him from the dead, you will be saved. For with the heart one believes unto righteousness, and with the mouth confession is made unto salvation" (NKJV). That's it! No trying to fix yourself. No getting your act together before you do it—you just *do it!* You can't make yourself acceptable to God; you never could. The only way to do it is *His* way, which is Jesus.

You cannot get to heaven because of your own goodness; you can get there because of God's goodness. All past, present, and future sin was judged at one time by God, placed on Jesus when He died on the cross. Because sin was judged, condemned, and paid for by Jesus, we don't have to pay for our own sin—it has already been paid for! You want to talk about good news? Now it's up to you to choose: Do you want to reject God's gift and pay the penalty for your sin, or do you want to receive Jesus?

If you're saying to yourself, "I want that!" then say this simple prayer aloud from your heart:

> *God, I repent of my sins. I believe Jesus came, died for my sins, rose from the dead on the third day, and is alive today. I confess with my mouth that Jesus is Lord, and according to your Word, I am now born again. I give all of my heart and all of my life to you now; and I receive your forgiveness, your cleansing, and eternal life—I'll never be the same. Thank you for changing me and washing me clean. In Jesus's name I pray. Amen.*

That's it! If you just said that prayer and believed it, you are now born again. You can write it down on your calendar. Today is your spiritual birthday! Congratulations! Now what do you do?

After you accept the Lord, I highly recommend that you find a good, Bible-based local church to get plugged into that can help disciple and grow you. It is *vitally* important that you now learn who you are in Christ. Everything God promised you in Christ is now yours, but if you don't know what that means, you can't take advantage of it. If you are having trouble finding a church, please contact me (contact@ effectivelivingllc.com), and I will do whatever I can to get you pointed in the right direction. There also are lots of great teaching resources that churches make available online, if you can't find something locally.

Bibliography

Allen, James. *As a Man Thinketh*. Wildside Press, LLC.

Autry, James A. *The Servant Leader: How to Build a Creative Team, Develop Great Morale, and Improve Bottom-Line Performance*. New York: Three Rivers Press, 2001.

Blue Letter Bible, s.v. "Hebrews 10:23" (KJV). Accessed December 3, 2016. https://www.blueletterbible.org/lang/lexicon/lexicon.cfm?strongs=G1680.

Bolton, Robert. *People Skills: How to Assert Yourself, Listen to Others, and Resolve Conflicts*. New York: Simon & Schuster, 1986.

Carnegie, Dale. *How to Win Friends and Influence People*. Simon & Schuster hardcover ed. New York: Simon & Schuster, 2009.

Covey, Stephen R. *The 7 Habits of Highly Effective People: Powerful Lessons in Personal Change*. Free Press trade paperback ed. New York: Simon & Schuster, 2004.

Eastman, Blake. "How Much of Communication is Really Nonverbal?" The Nonverbal Group. Article published August 2011. http://www.nonverbalgroup.com/2011/08/how-much-of-communication-is-really-nonverbal.

Giblin, Les. *How to Have Confidence and Power in Dealing with People*. New York: Prentice Hall Press, 1956.

Giblin, Les. *Skill with People*. Rev. ed. 2010.

Goleman, Daniel. "Daniel Goleman: Help Young Talent Develop a Professional Mindset." Article published September 13, 2015. http://www.danielgoleman.info/daniel-goleman-help-young-talent-develop-a-professional-mindset/.

Goleman, Daniel. *Emotional Intelligence*. Bantam trade paperback ed. 1997. New York: Bantam Books, 1997.

Goulston, Mark, and Philip Goldberg. *Get Out of Your Own Way: Overcoming Self-Defeating Behavior*. New York: Penguin Books, 1996.

Hendricksen, Dave. *12 Essential Skills for Software Architects*. Upper Saddle River, NJ: Addison-Wesley, 2011.

Hill, Napoleon. *Think and Grow Rich*. Meriden, CT: Ralston Society, 1937.

Jeffress, Robert. *When Forgiveness Doesn't Make Sense*. Colorado Springs, CO: WaterBrook Press, 2000.

Navarro, Joe, and Marvin Karlins. *What Every BODY Is Saying: An Ex-FBI Agent's Guide to Speed-Reading People*. New York: HarperCollins Publishers, 2008.

Yager, Dexter, and Ron Ball. *Dynamic People Skills: Developing Relationships that Develop Success*. InterNET Services Corporation, 1997.

Made in the USA
San Bernardino, CA
19 March 2017